Twisted

Twisted

A Series of Entwined Graphite Drawings

William Oliver Reed

To order additional copies of this book, contact:
Xlibris Corporation
1-888-795-4274
www.Xlibris.com
Orders@Xlibris.com
70131

This book is dedicated to my late wife Rachael.

This series came flowing out of me from 1998 until the end of 2003. These graphite drawings are the result of searching for a way to deal with mounting problems. Each piece is unique, completely different from the next, but at the same time, exactly the same. I like to plant little subtle drawings within the drawing to further intrigue the viewer. Look for the faces and figures in some of the drawings trees and branches. Think about the captions for further insight. Stare into the drawings and see what you can see!

Art won't hurt you! Enjoy.

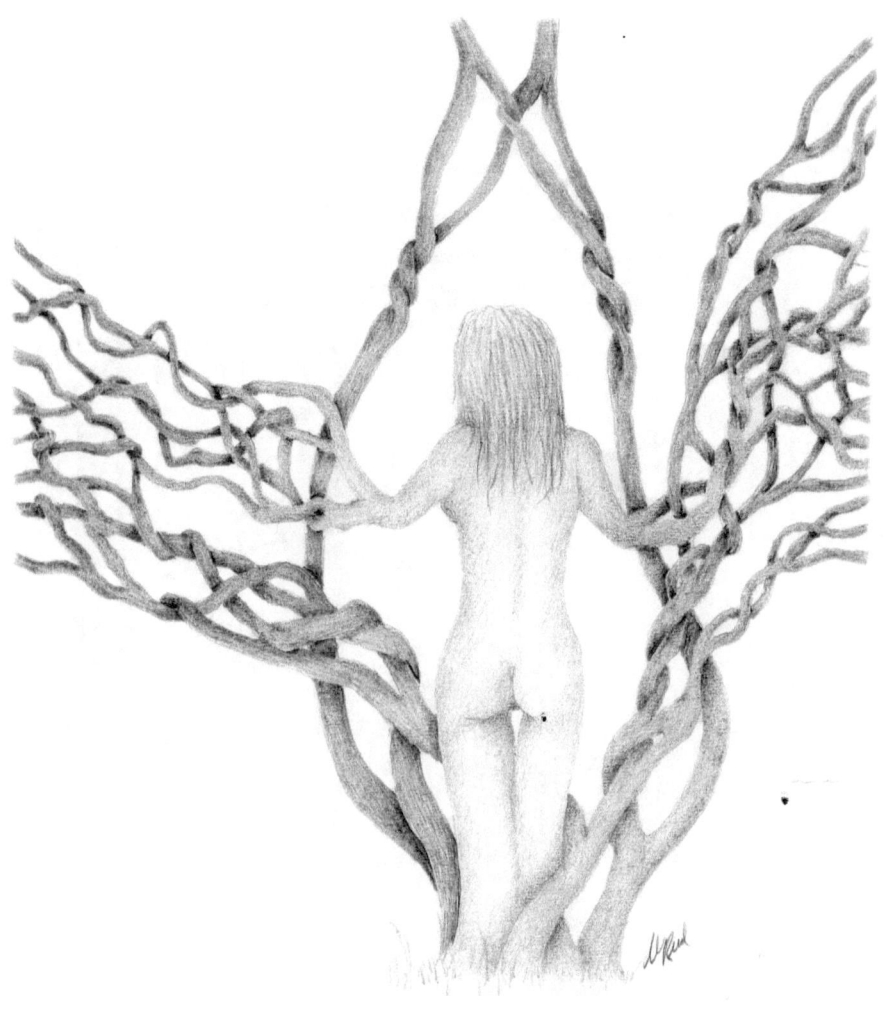

Birth of Eve

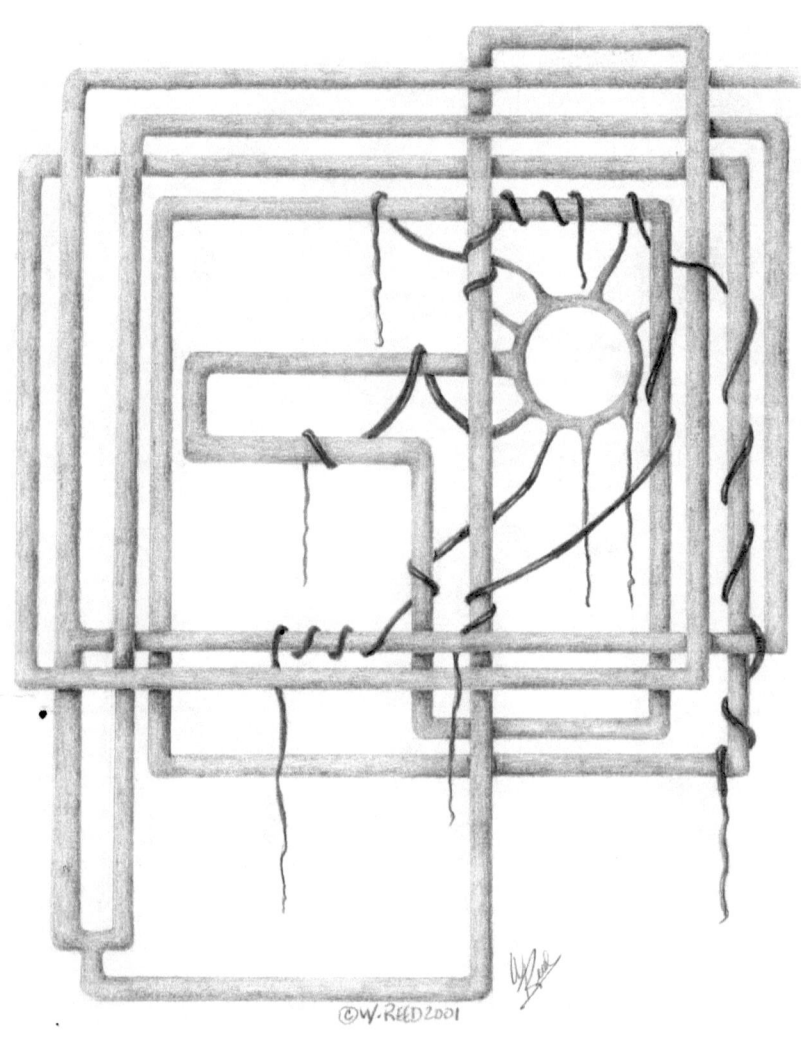

Art Can't Hurt You

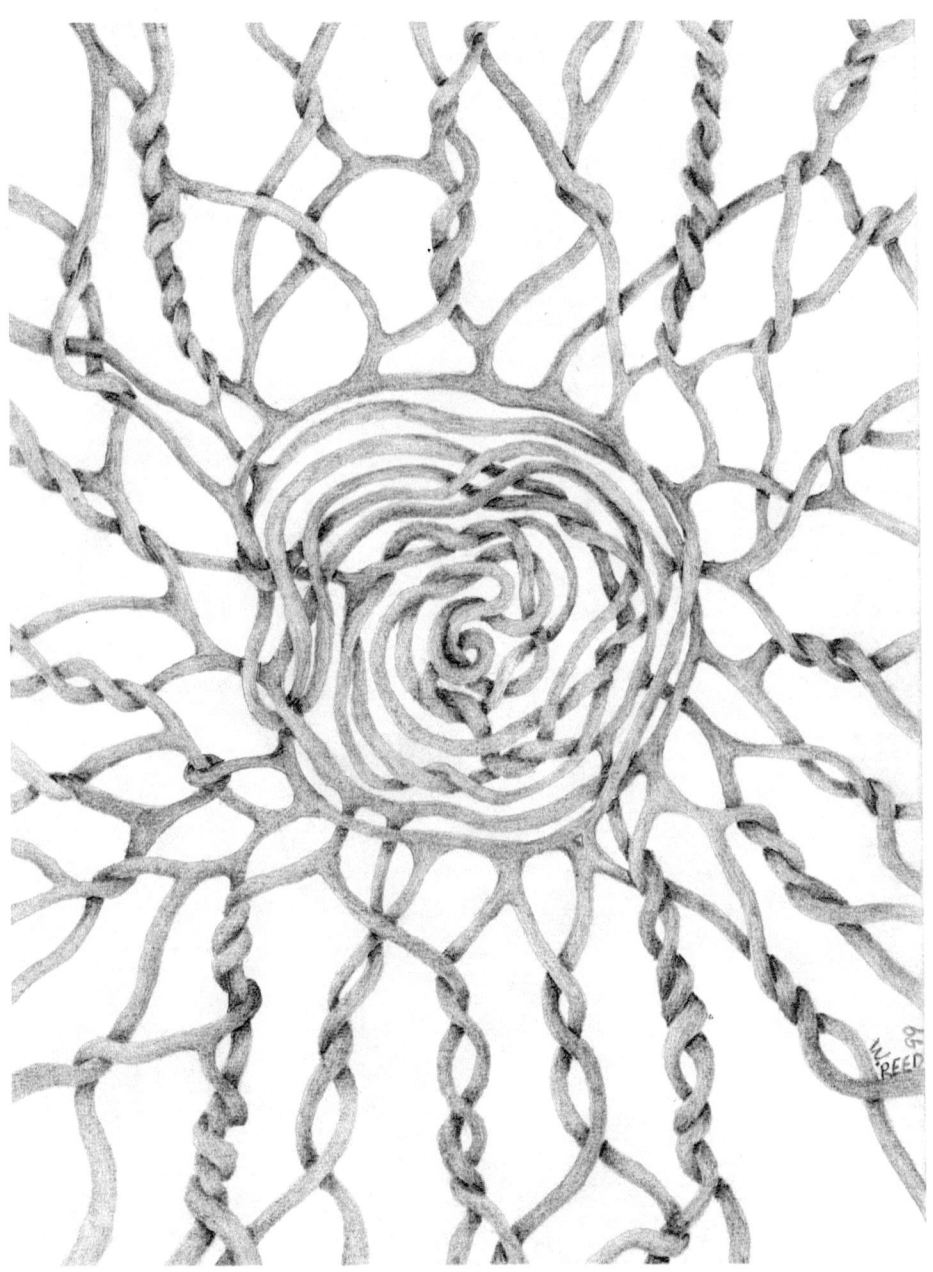

Circular Vine

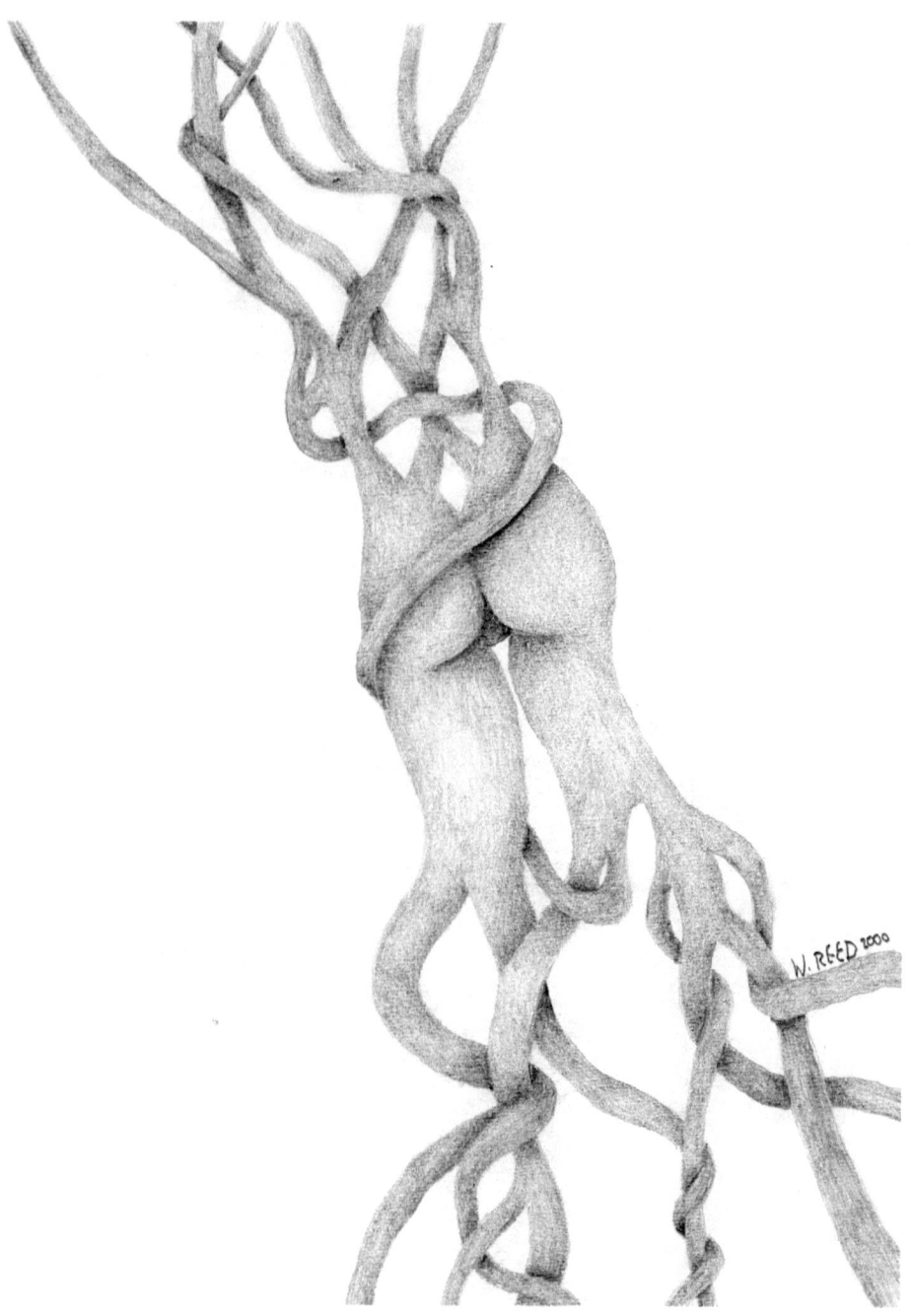

Typical Day in Life

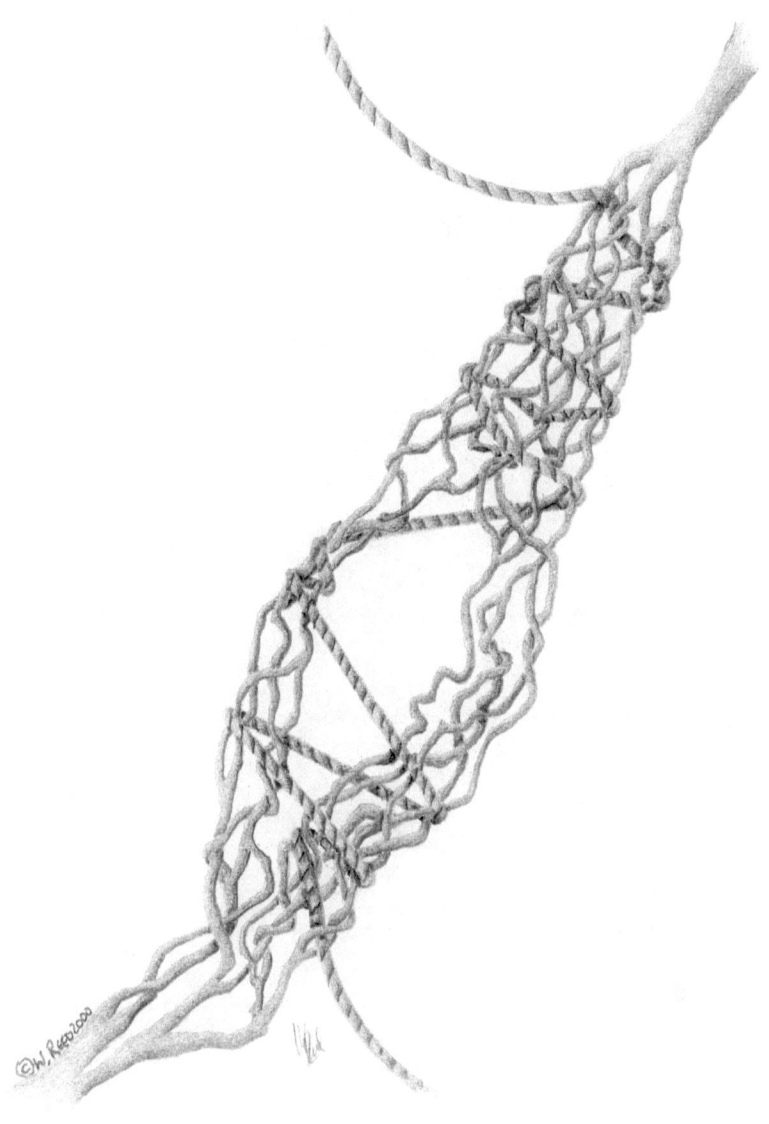

Contemplating Life

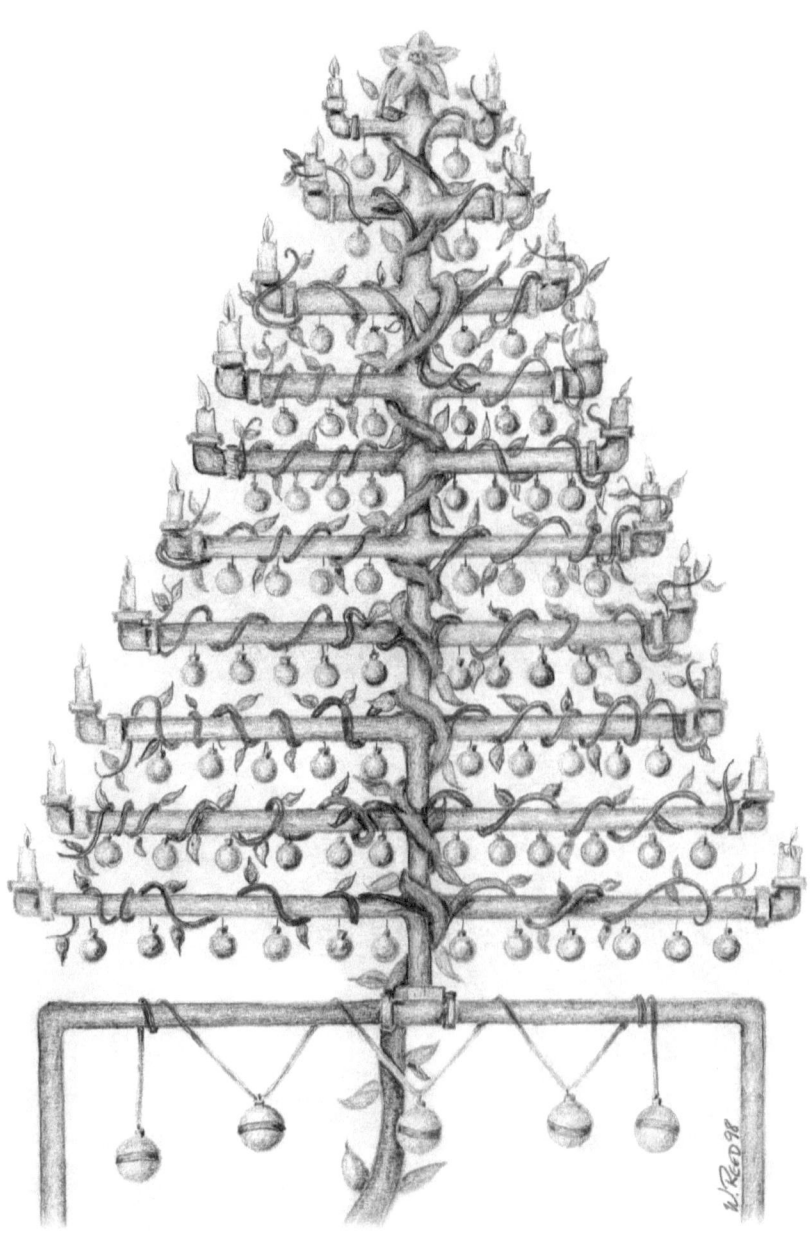

Christmas Card 99

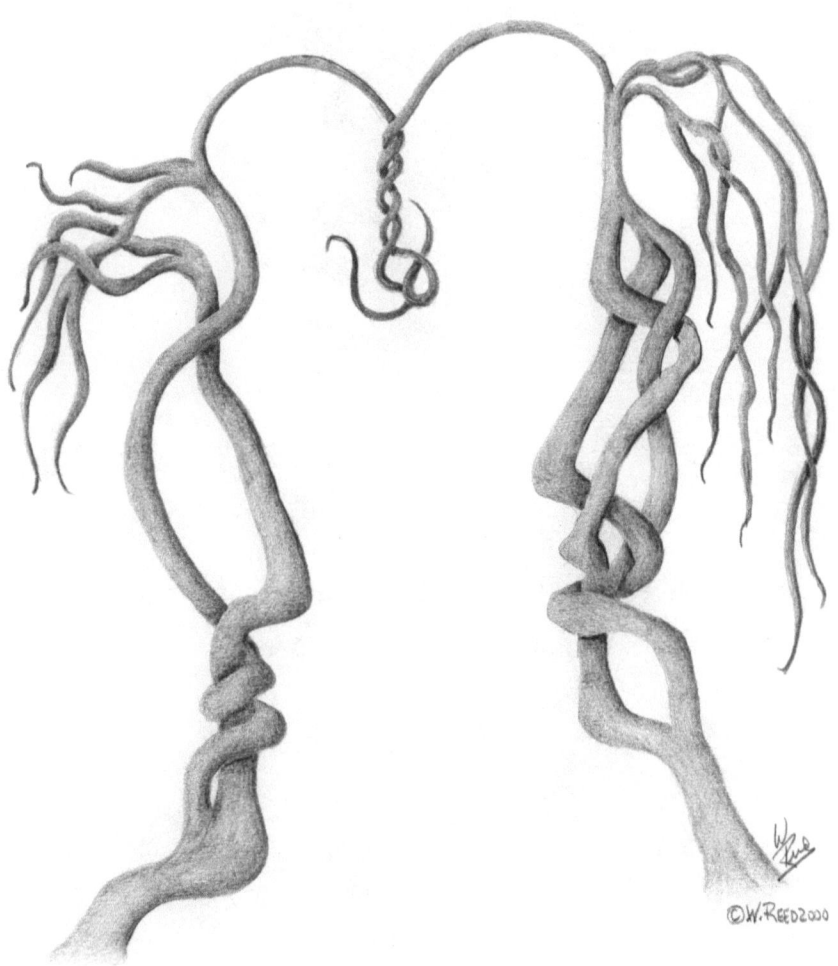

Contemplating Marriage

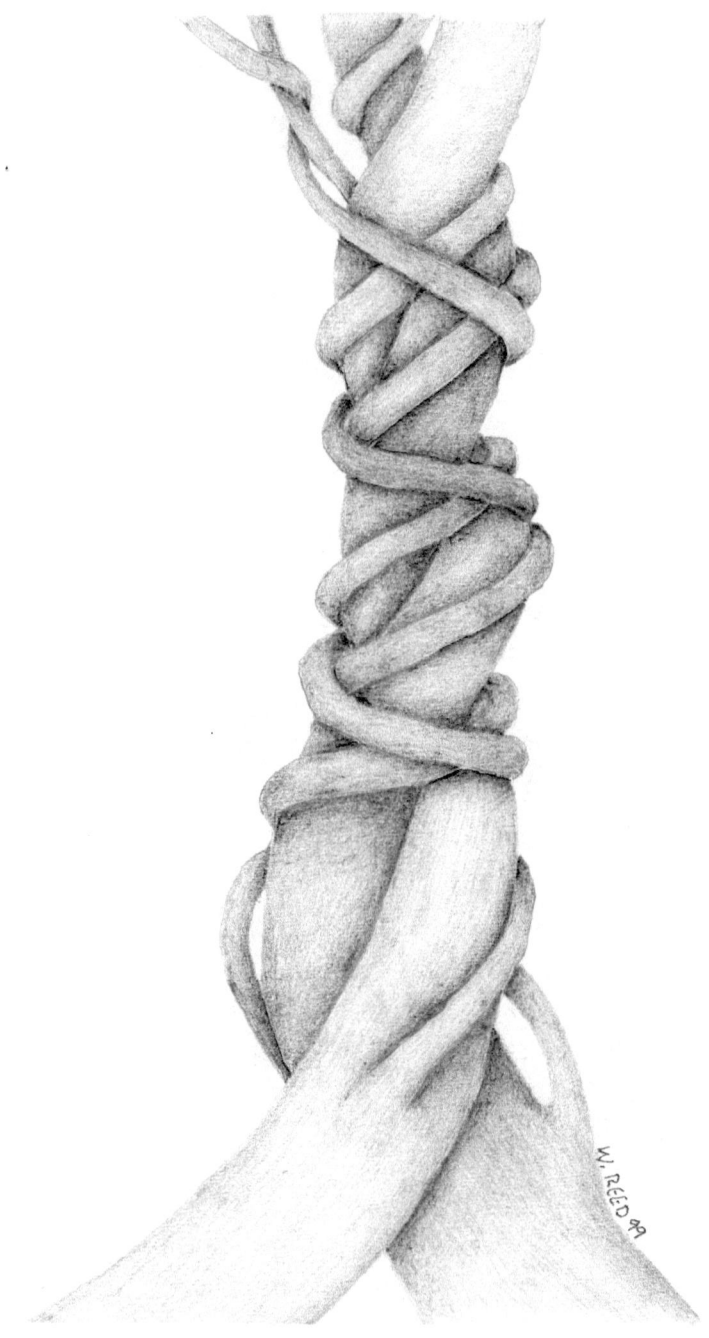

The Hug

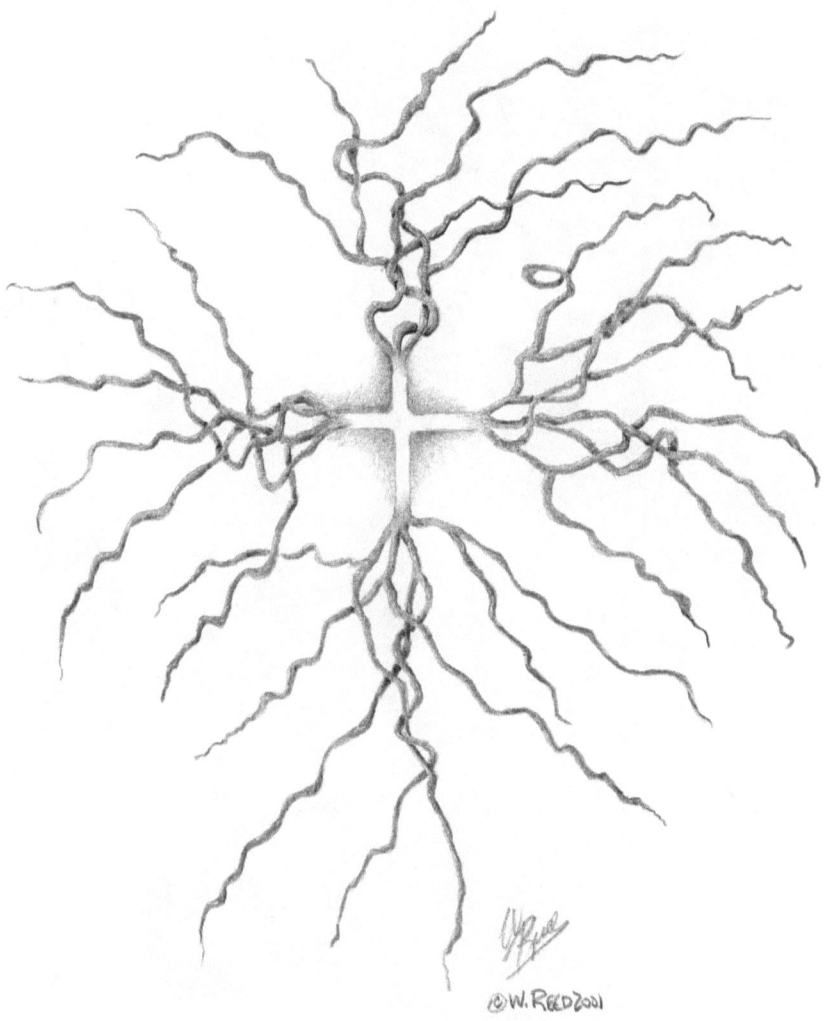

Crossroads

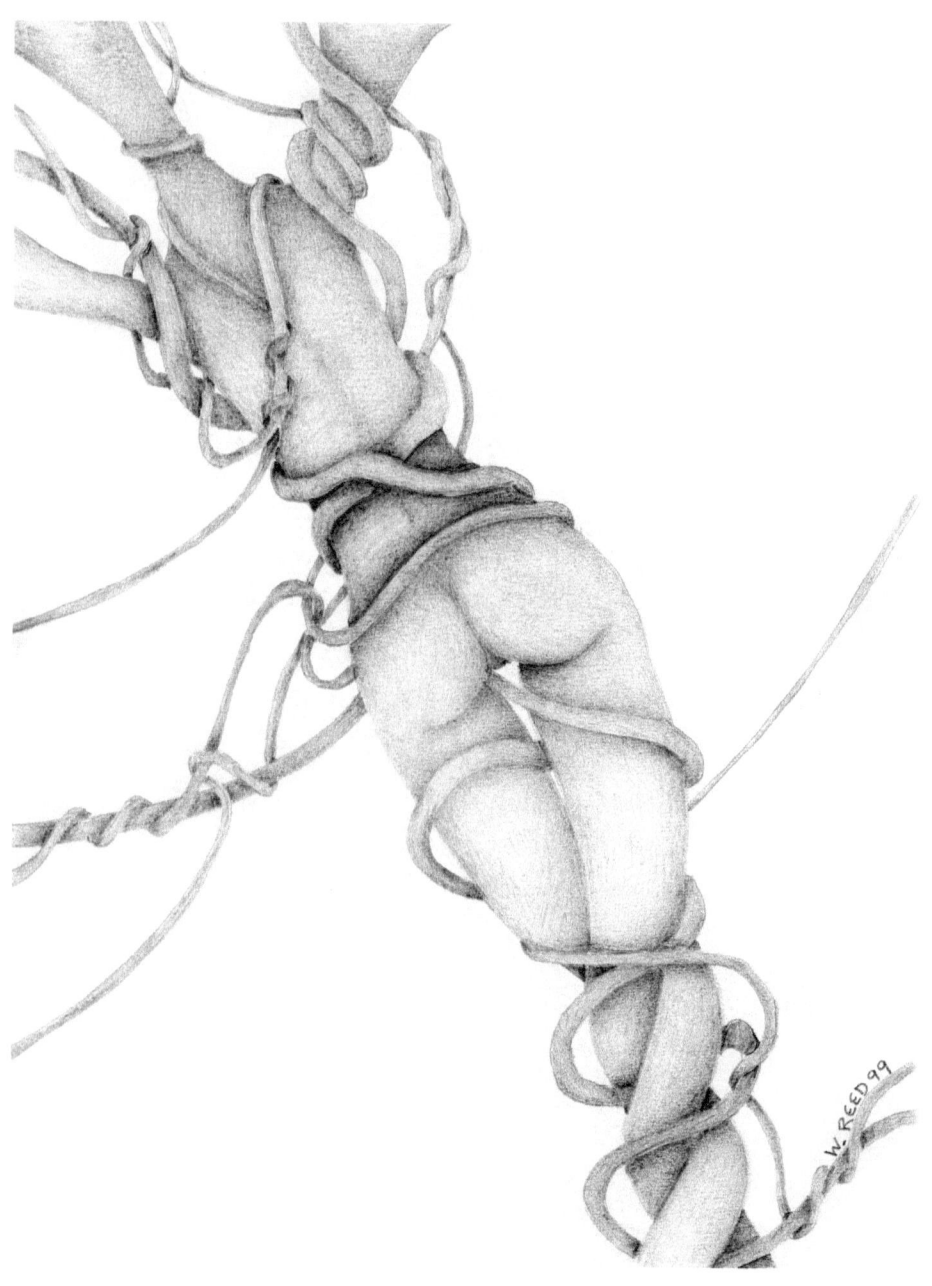

Eroticadram

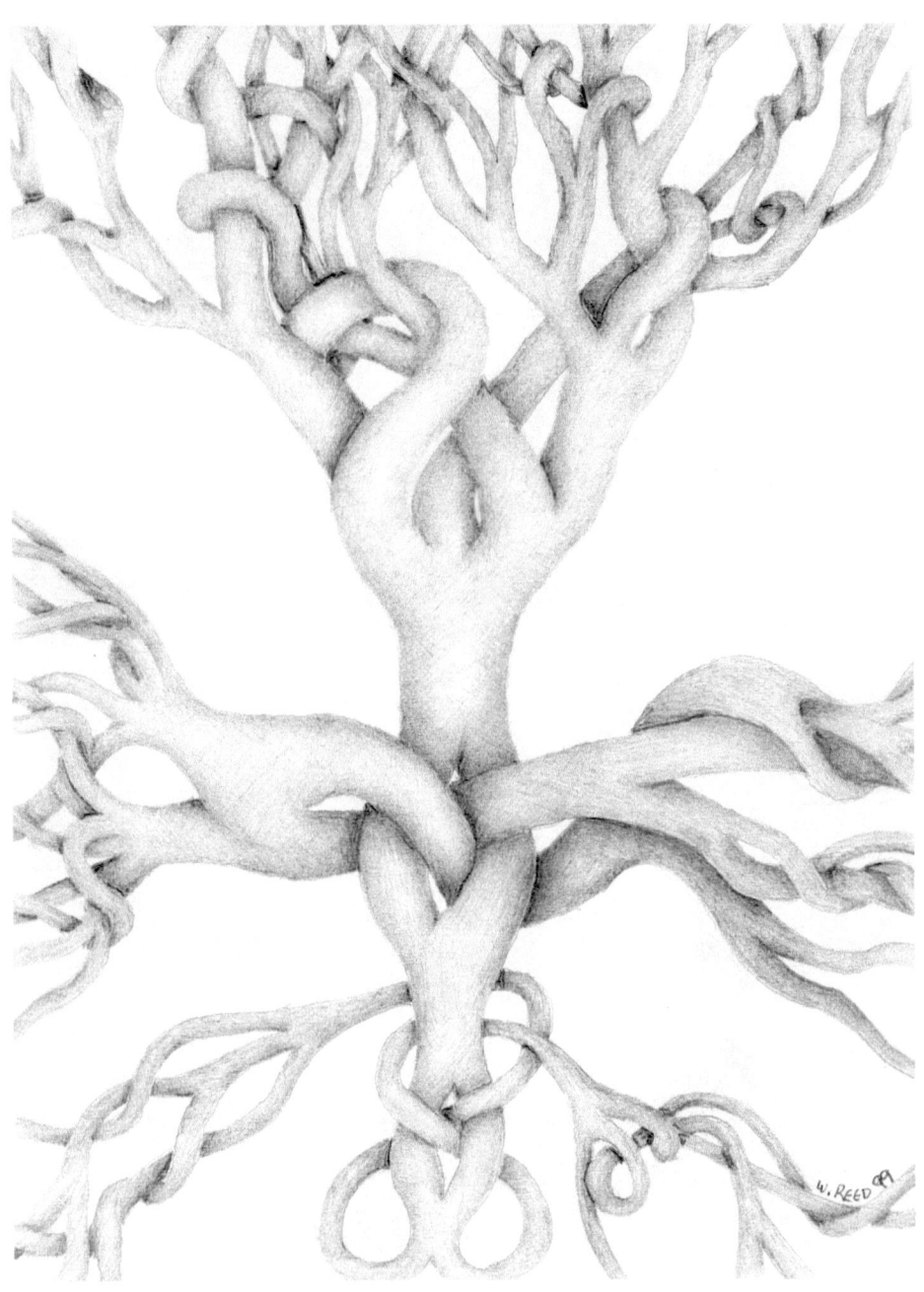

Crosstree

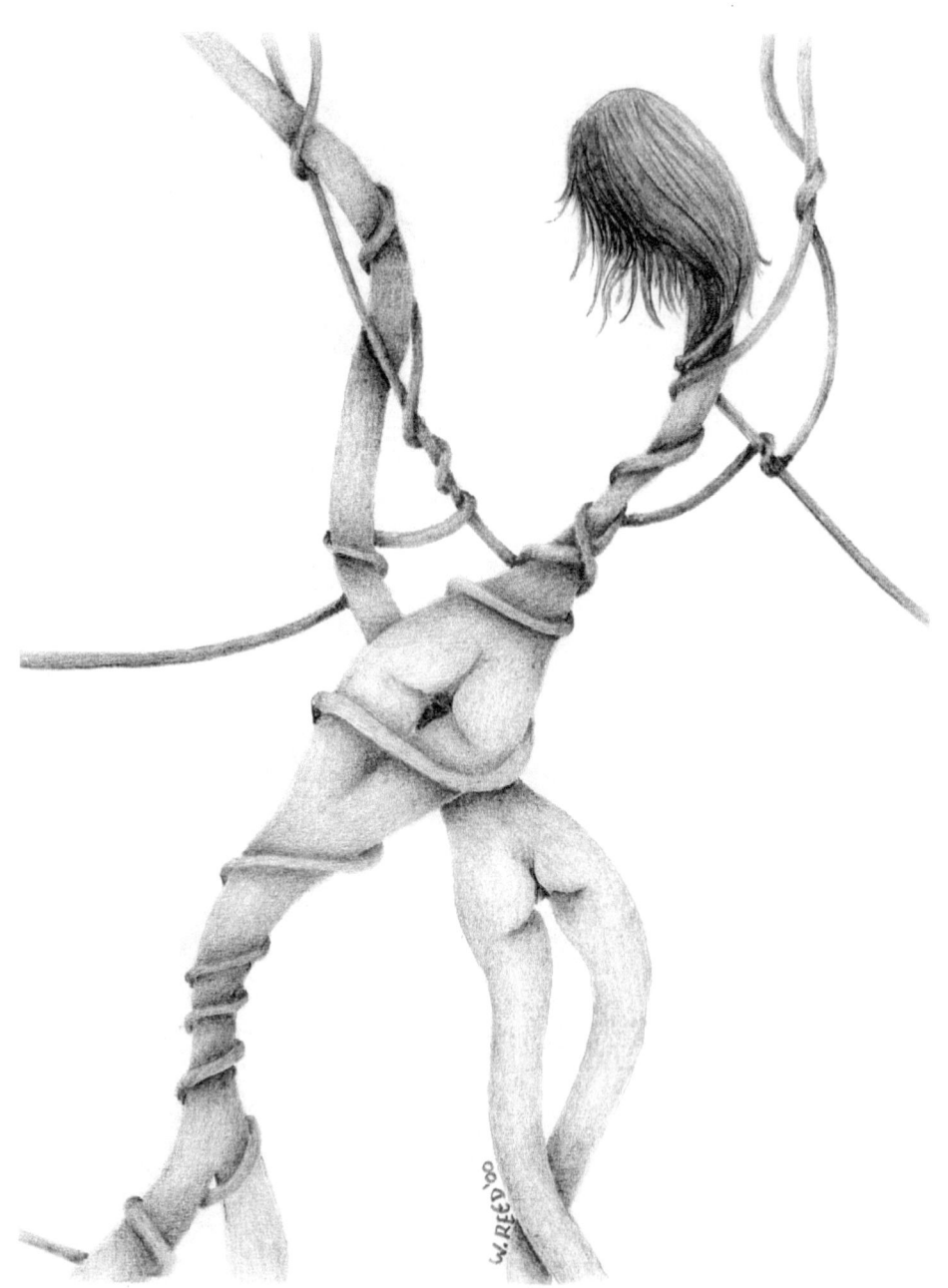

Cat Fight

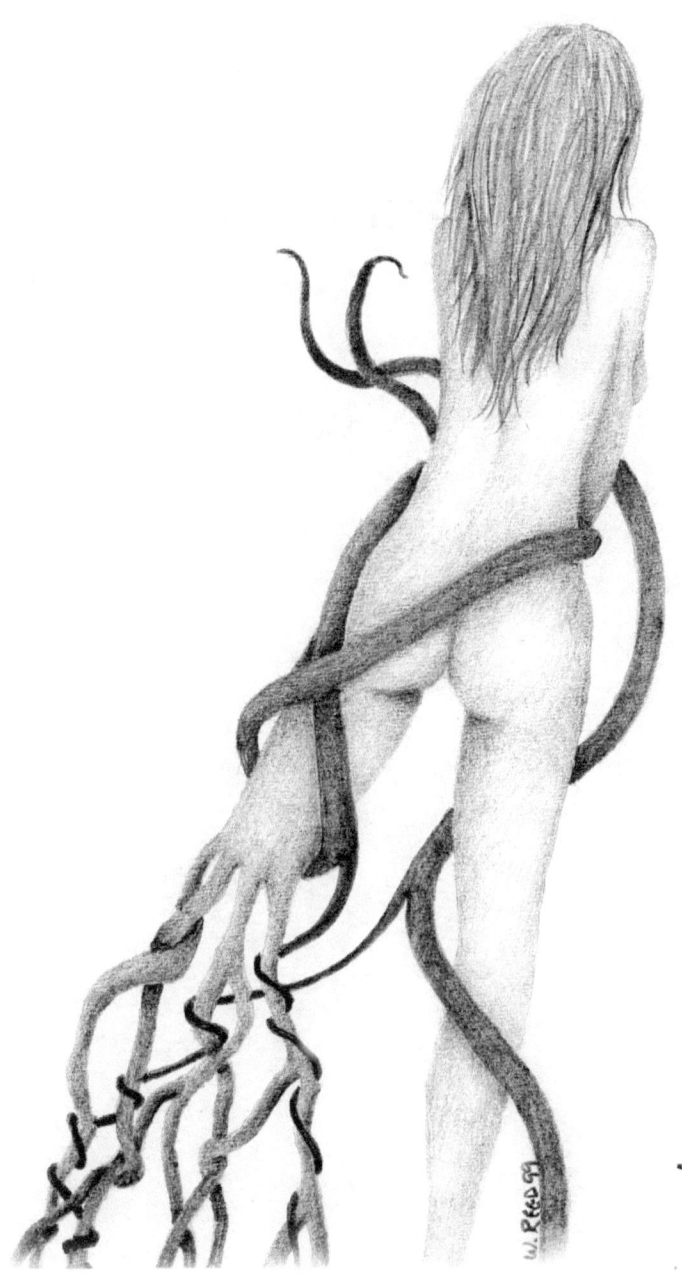

Motherhood

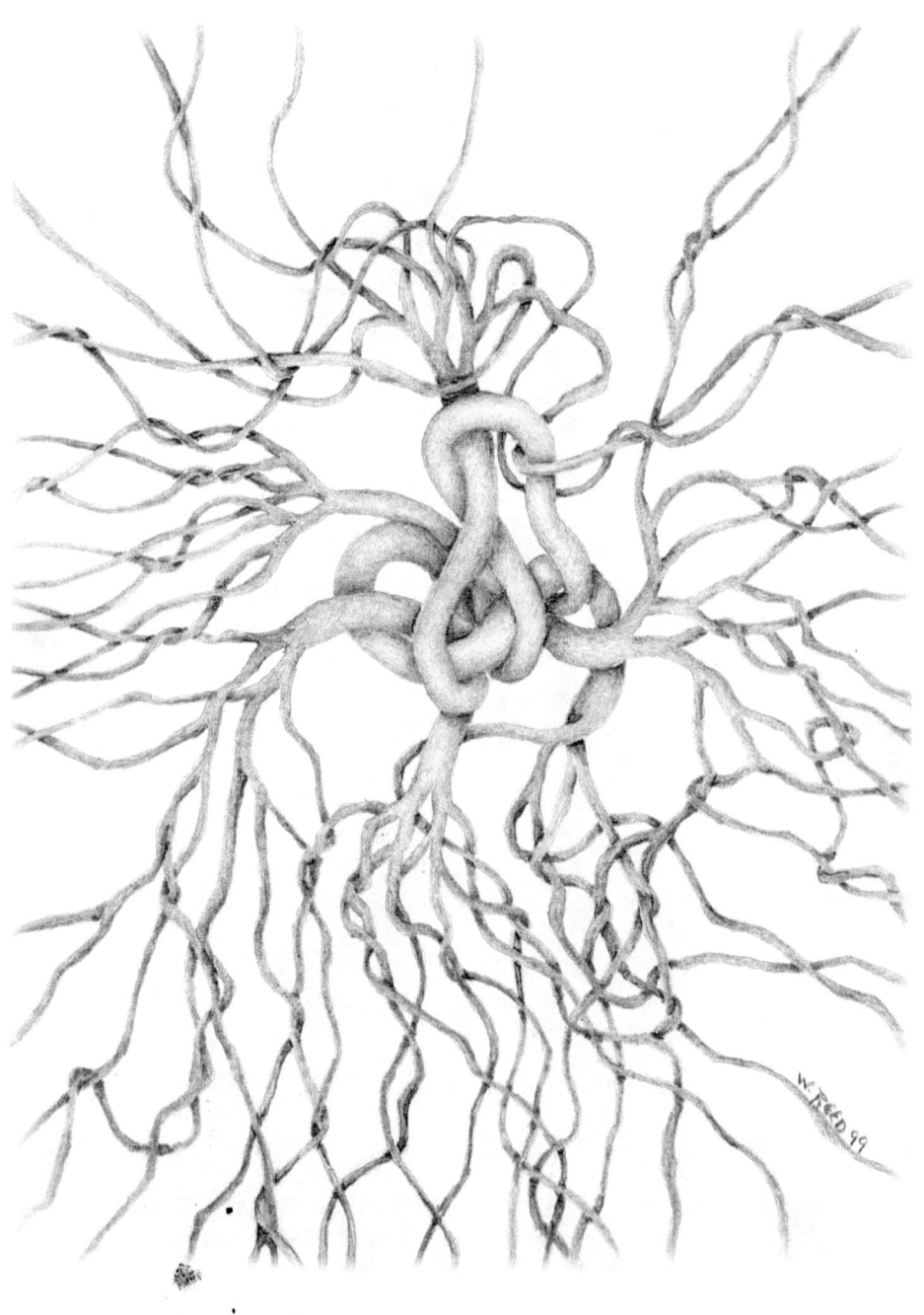

Aorta

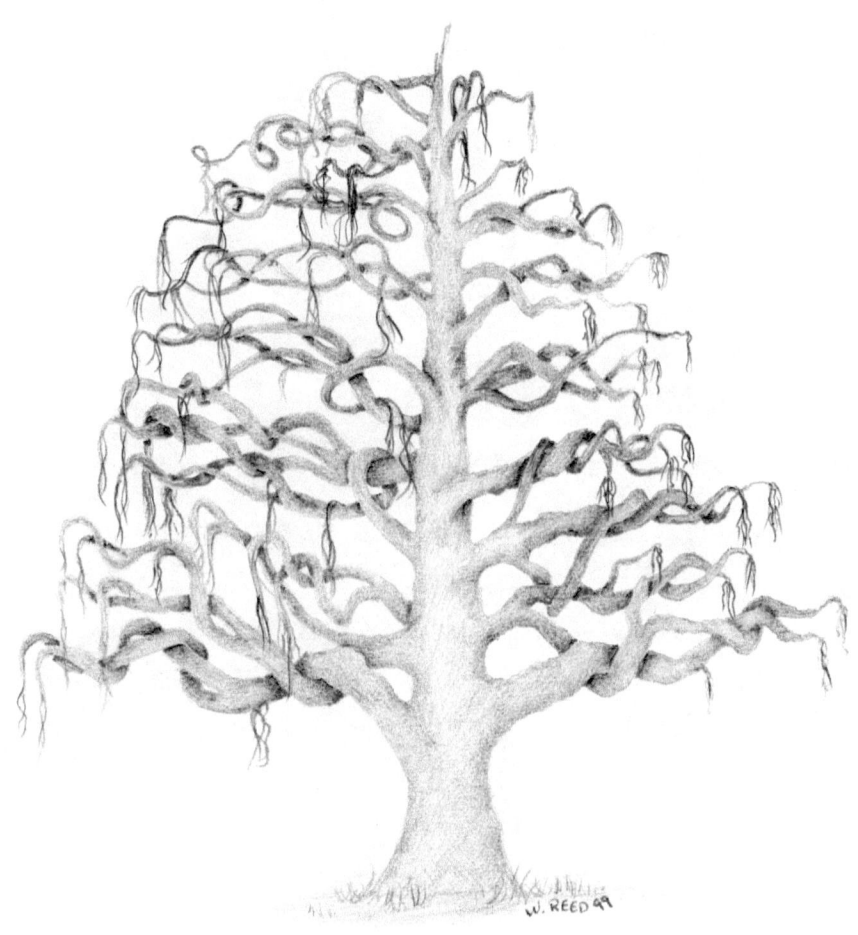

Just a tree

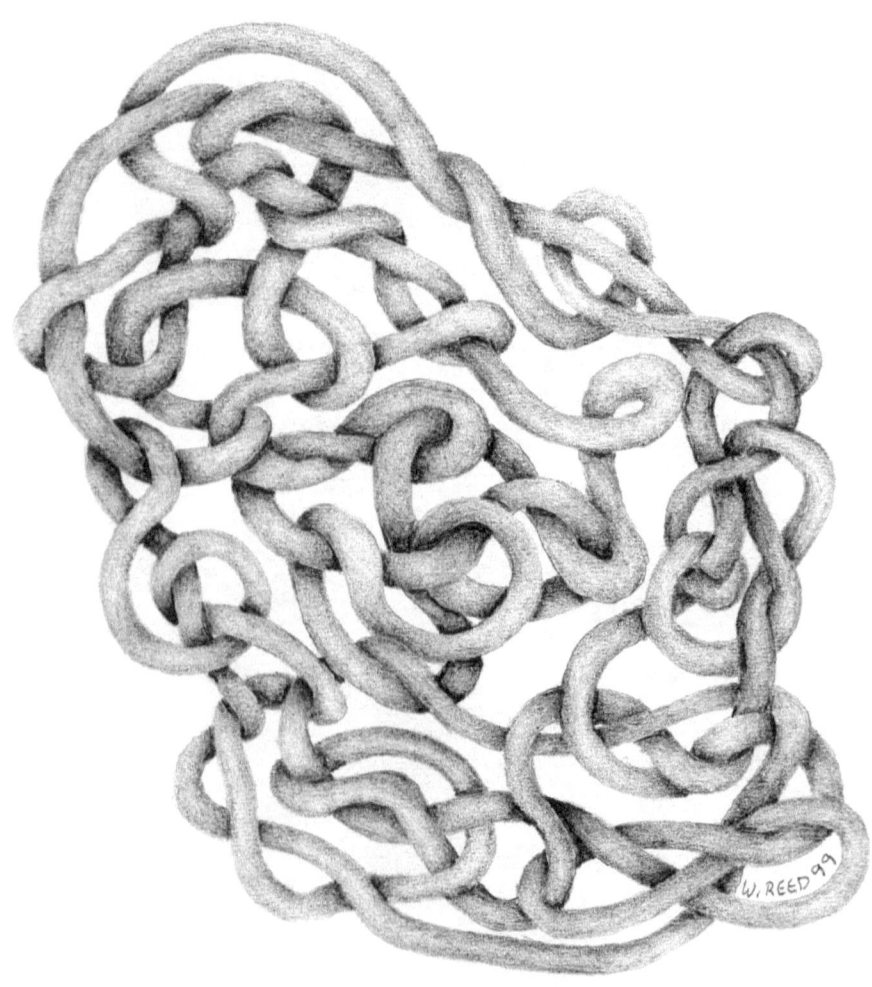

Continuem

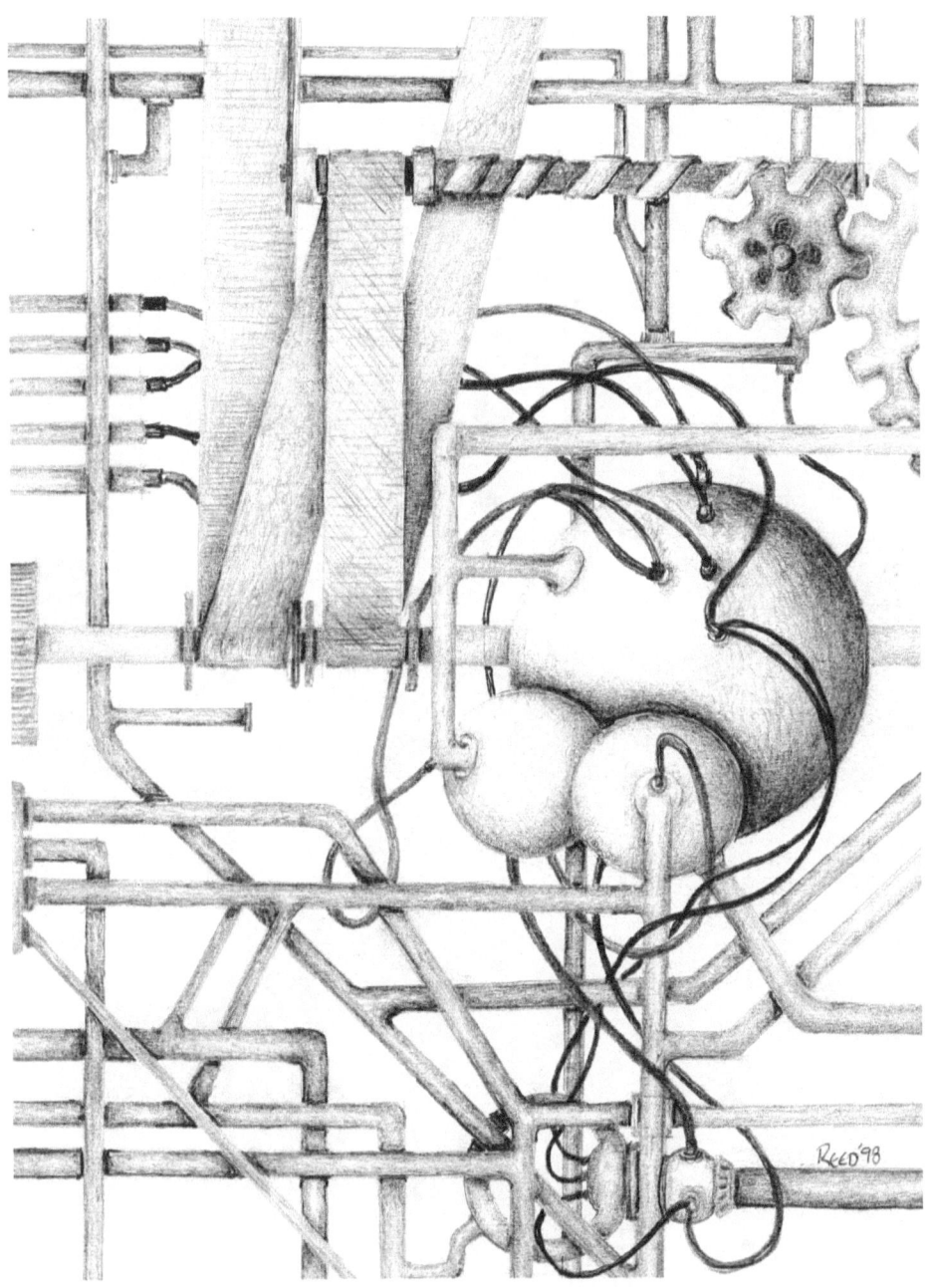

Mechanics

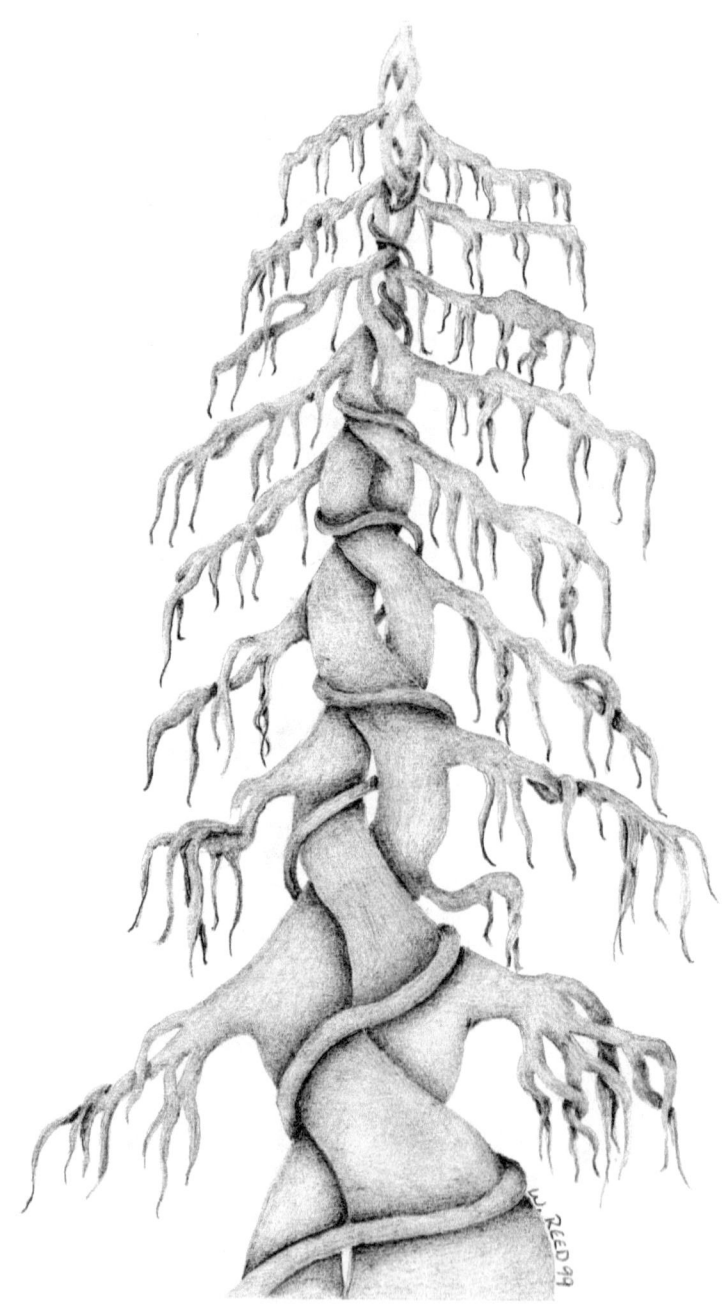

Demon Tree

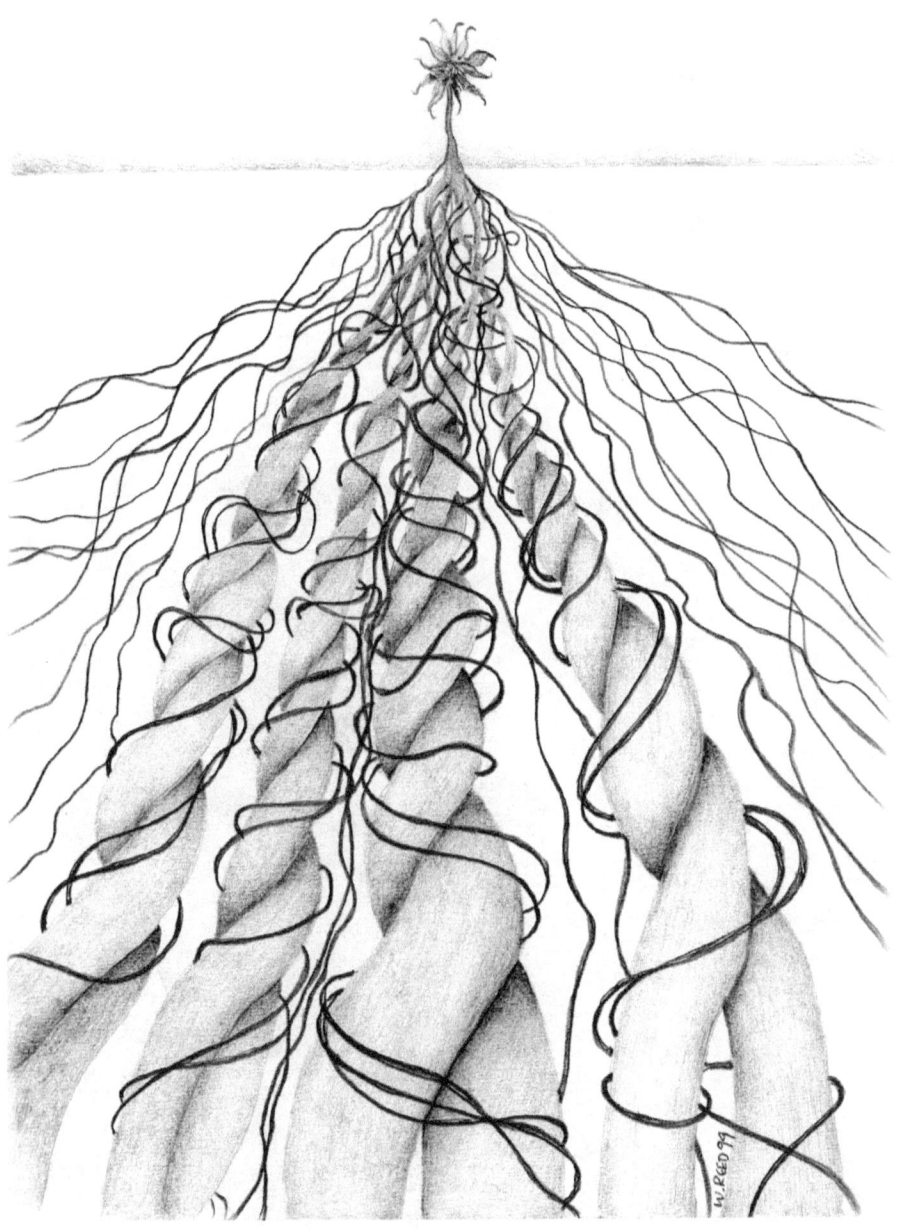

Roots 2

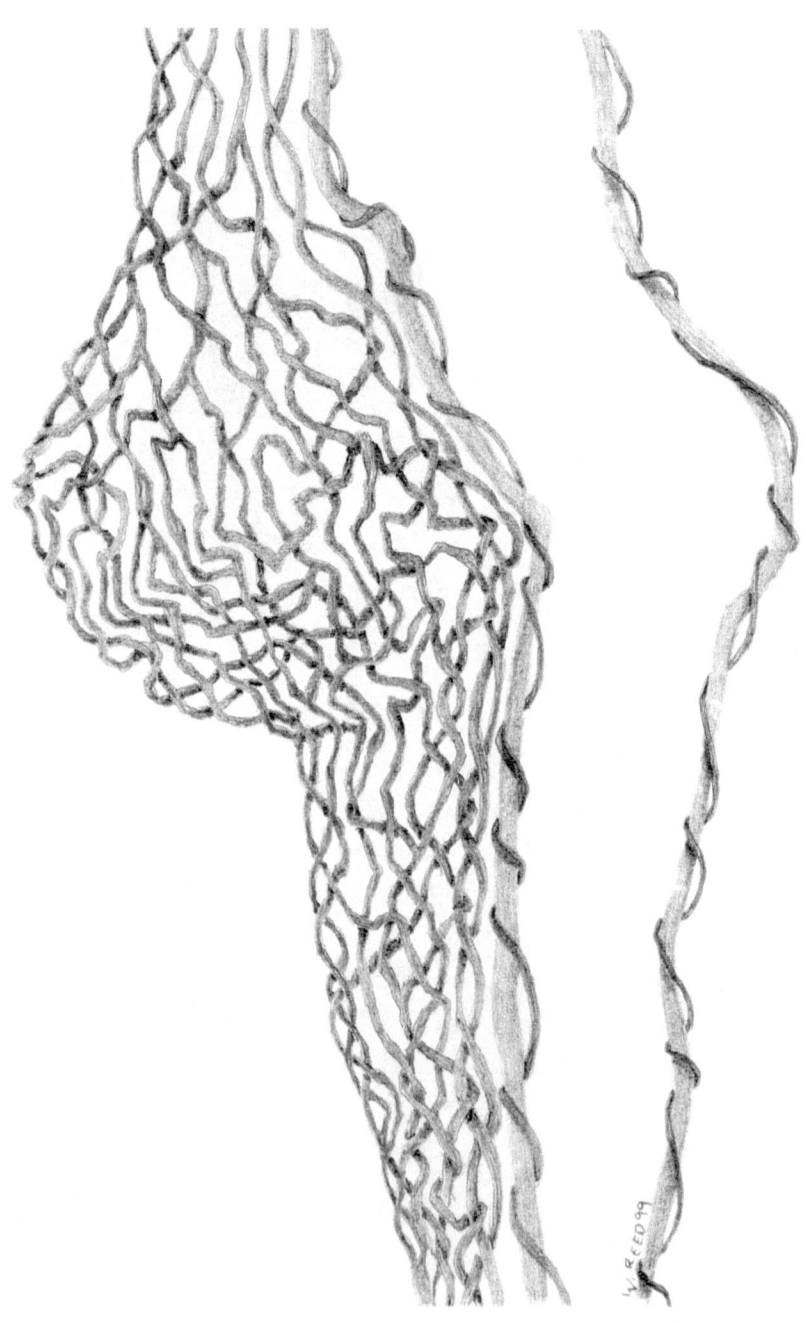

Woman

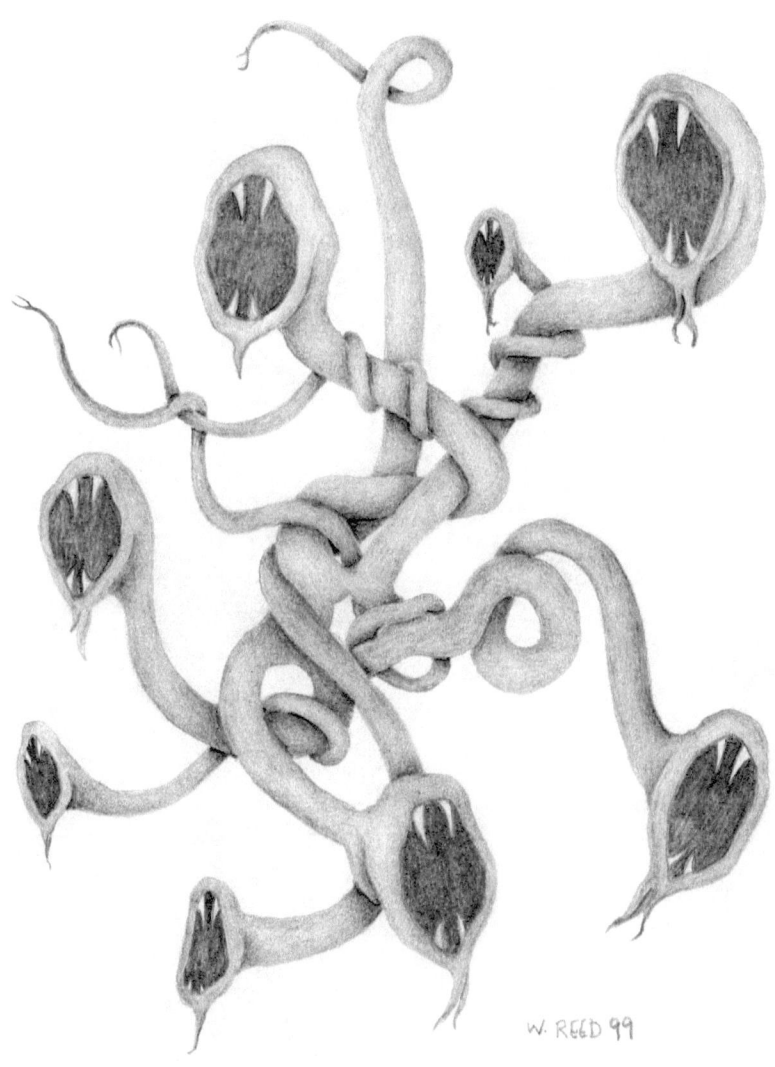

Eyeless Snakes

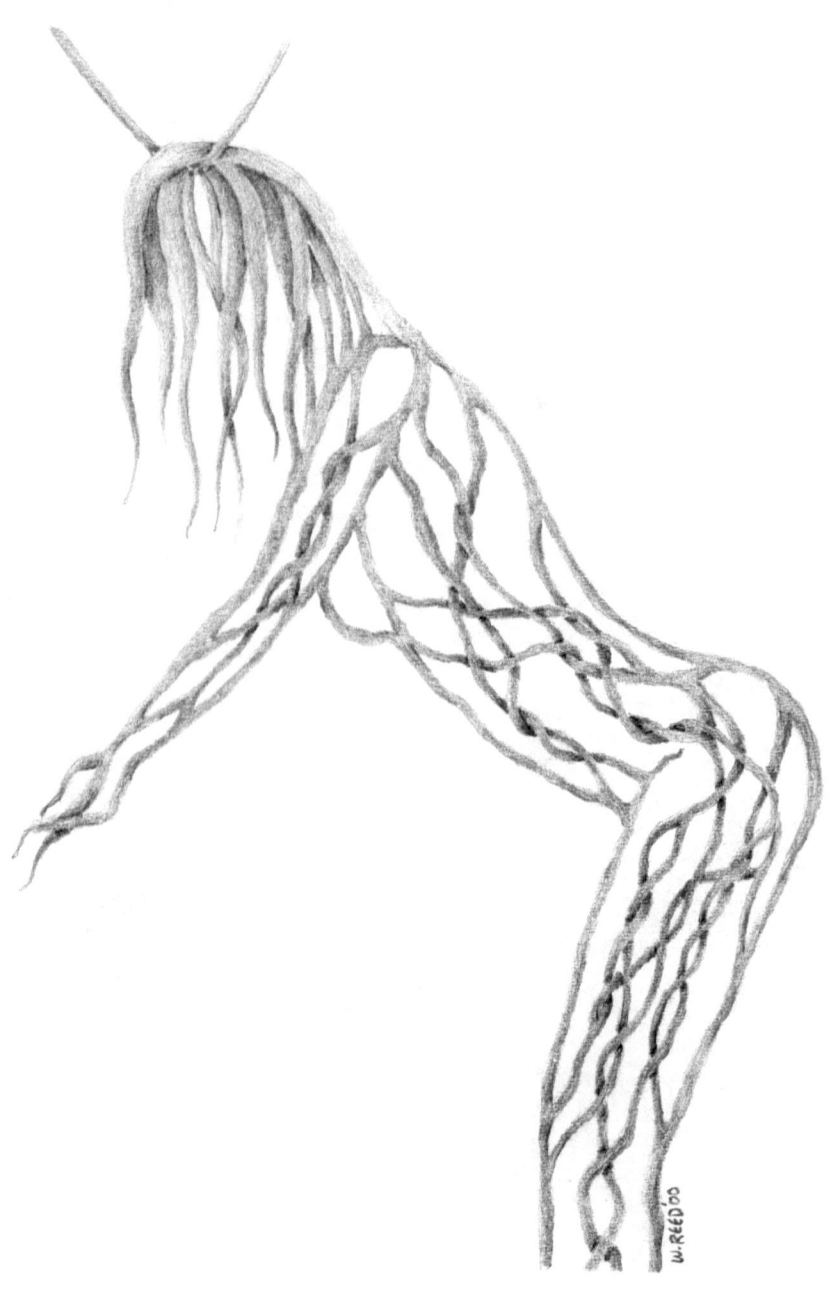

Developing

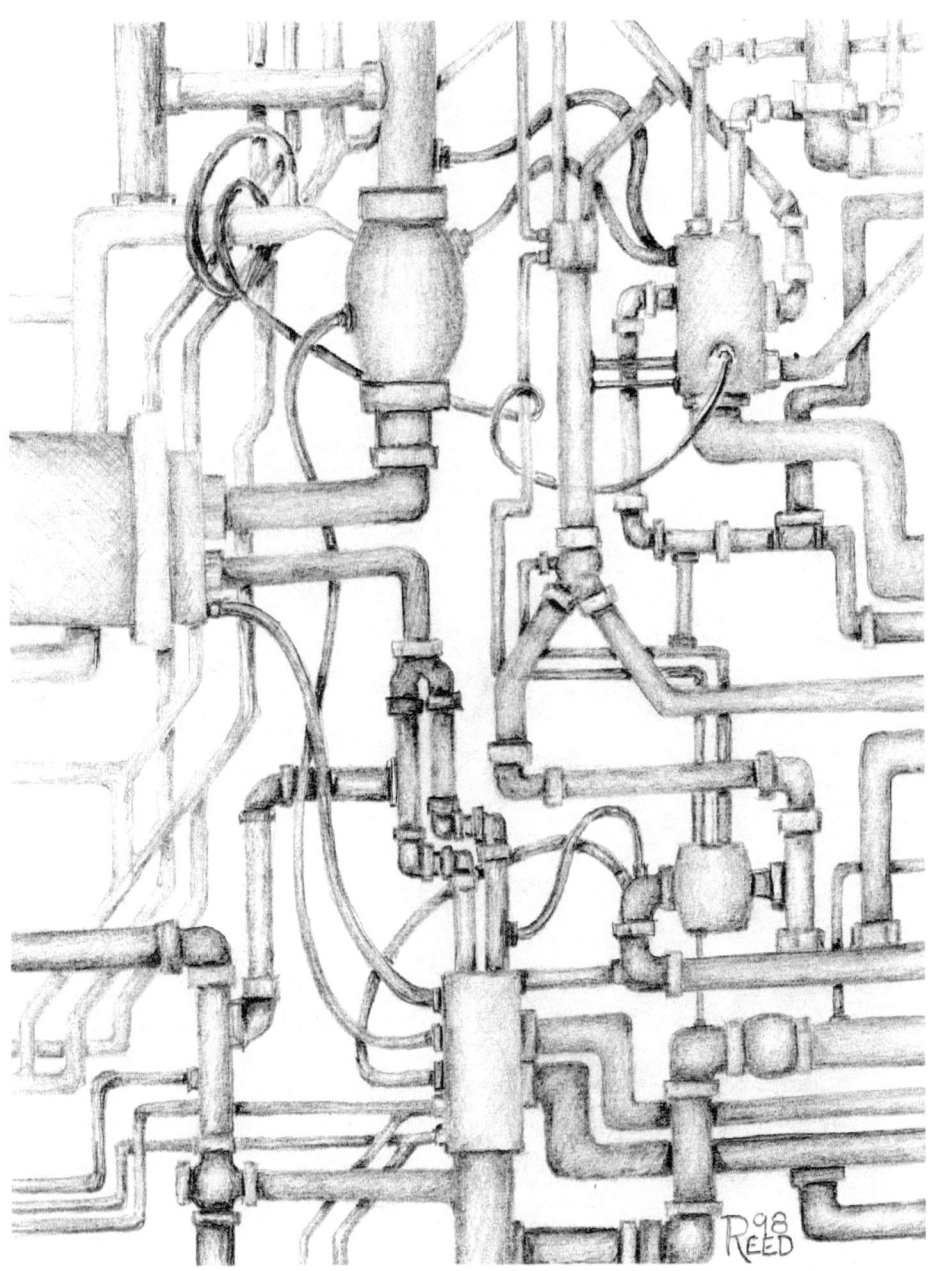

Under Pressure

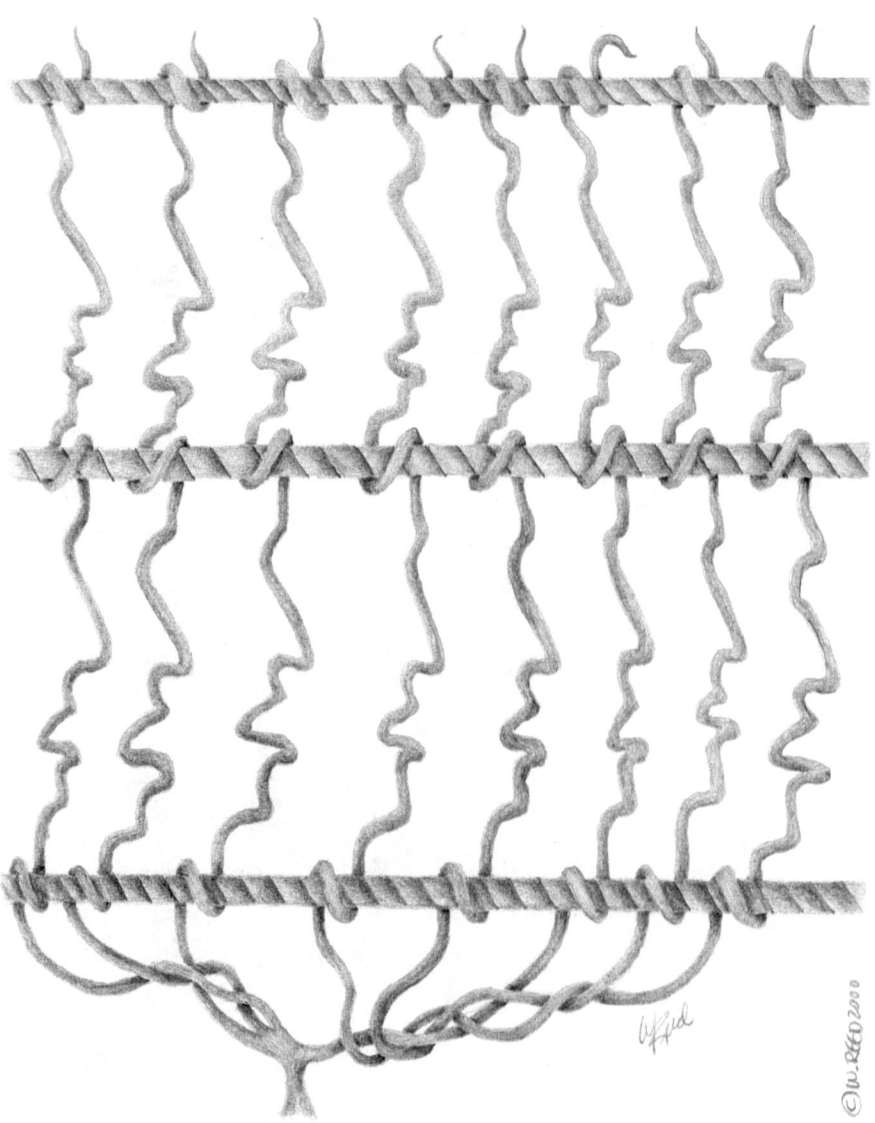

16 Thoughts

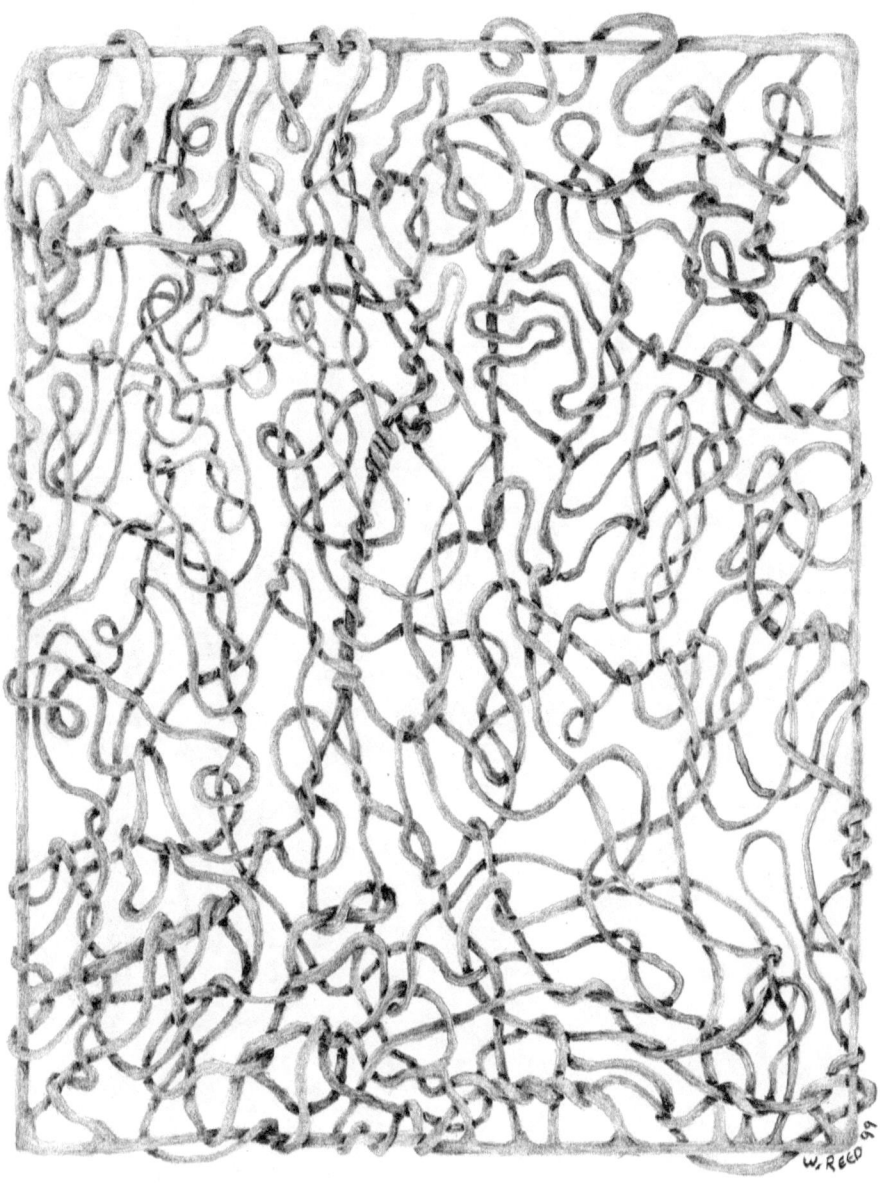

Vicissitudes

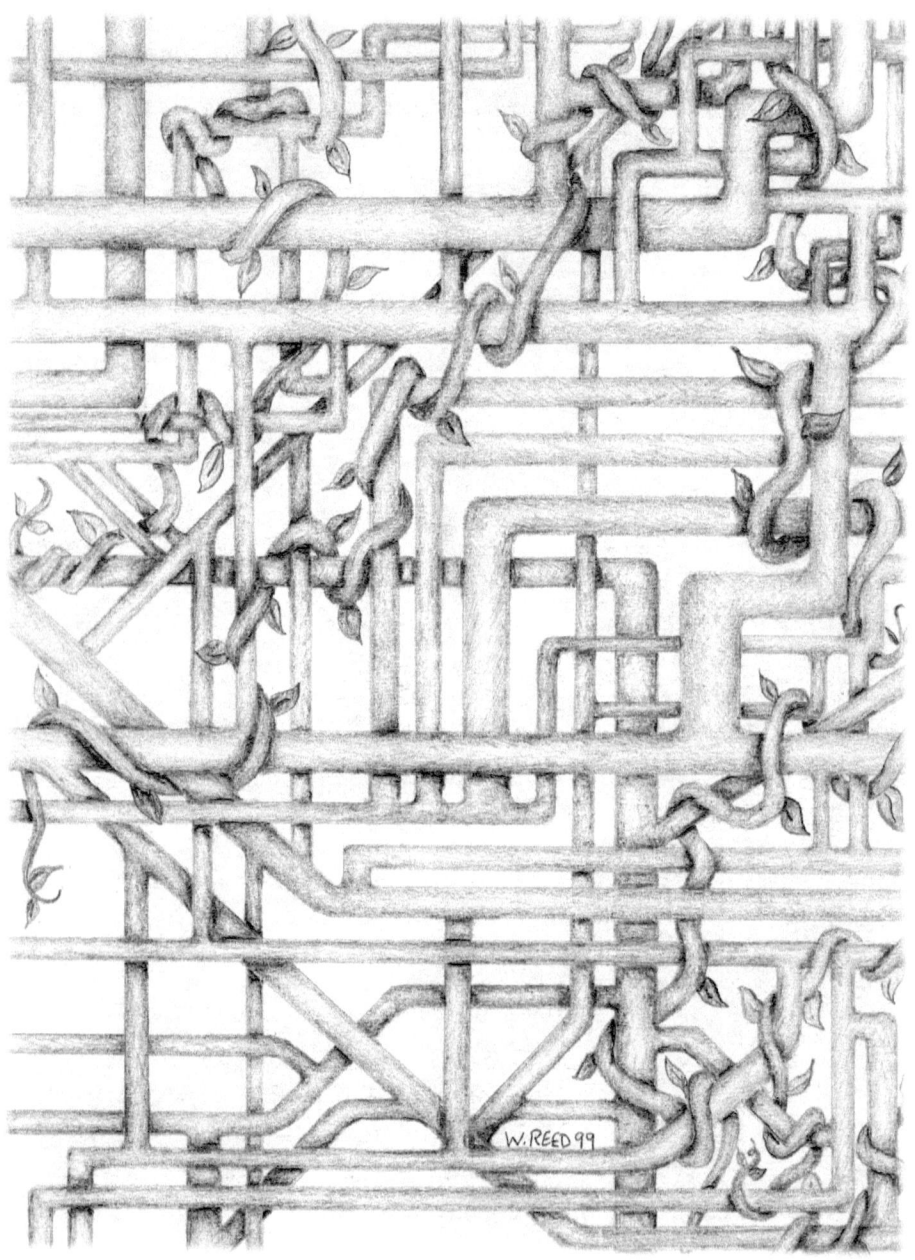

Pipes & Vines

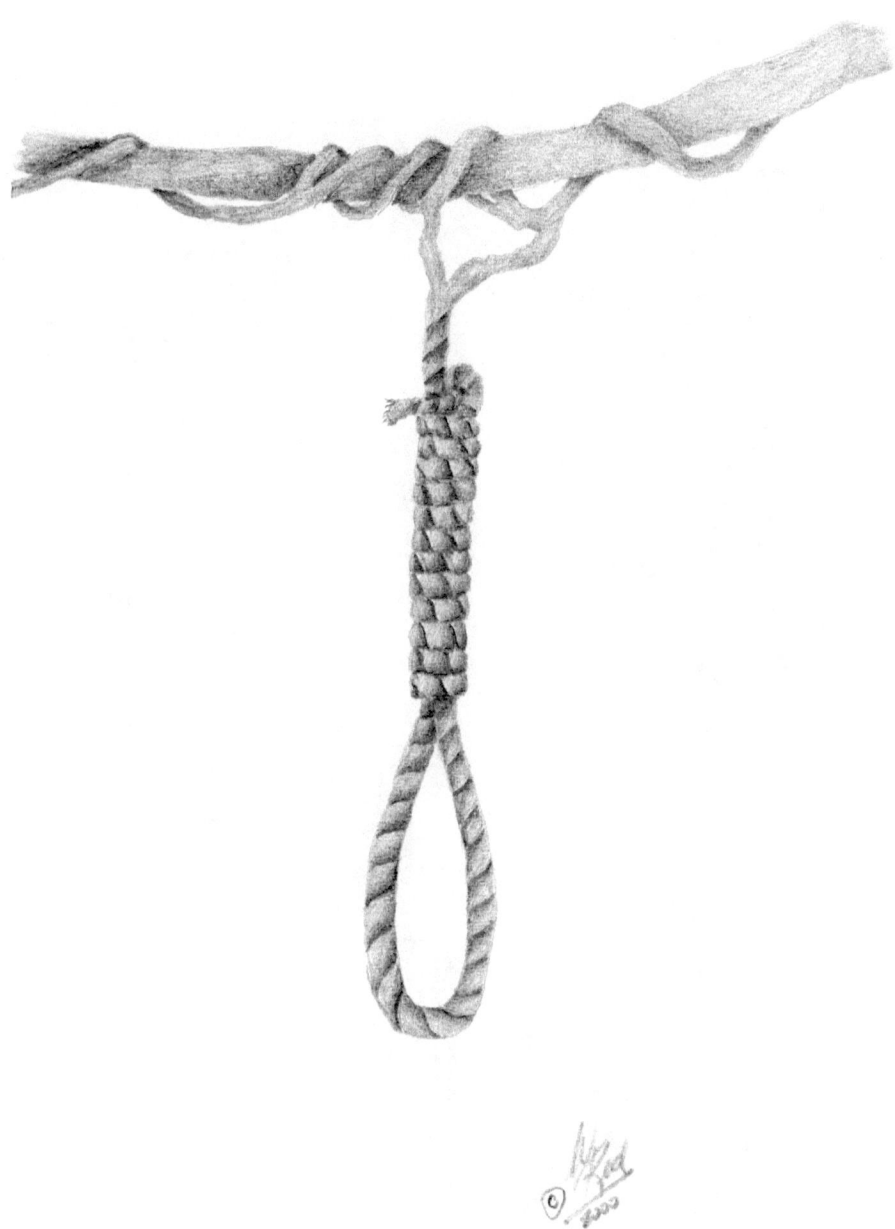

Vine to Noose

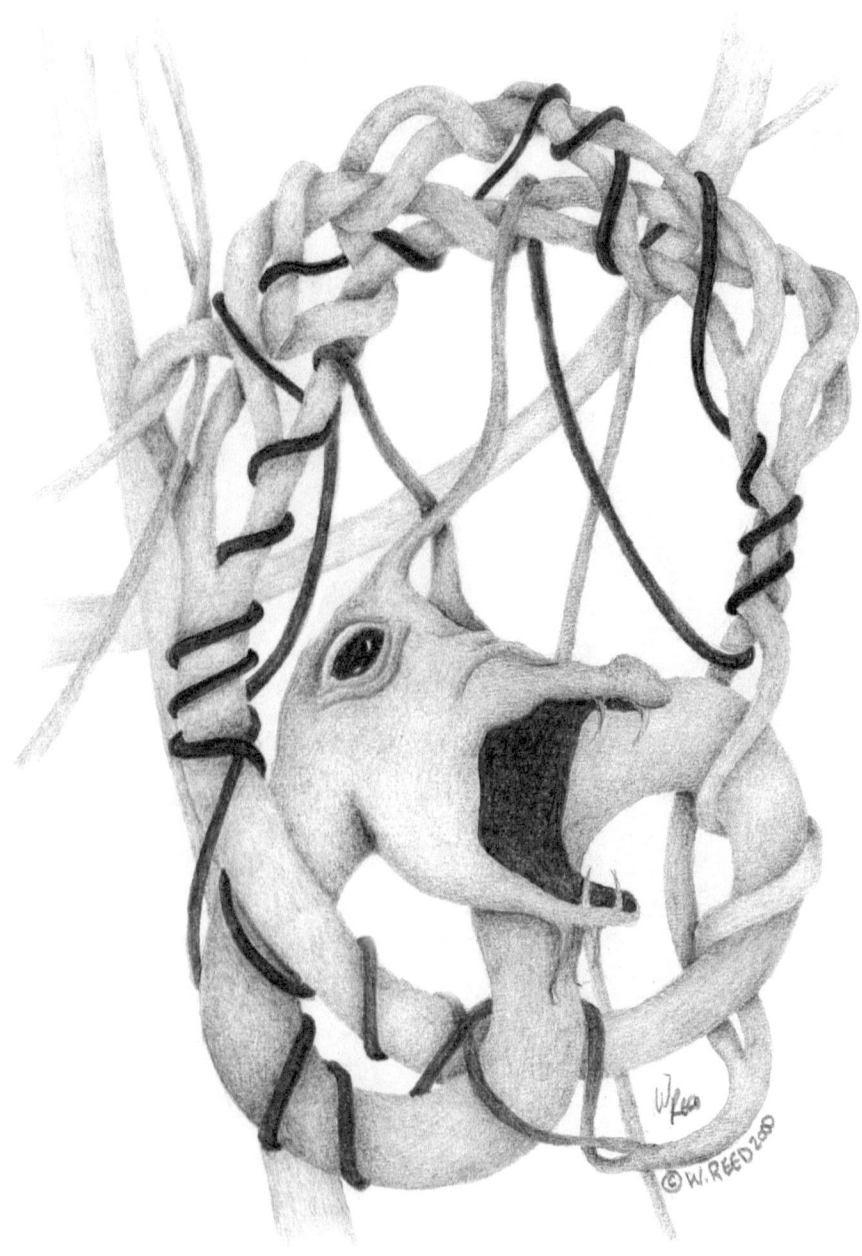

Archrillias

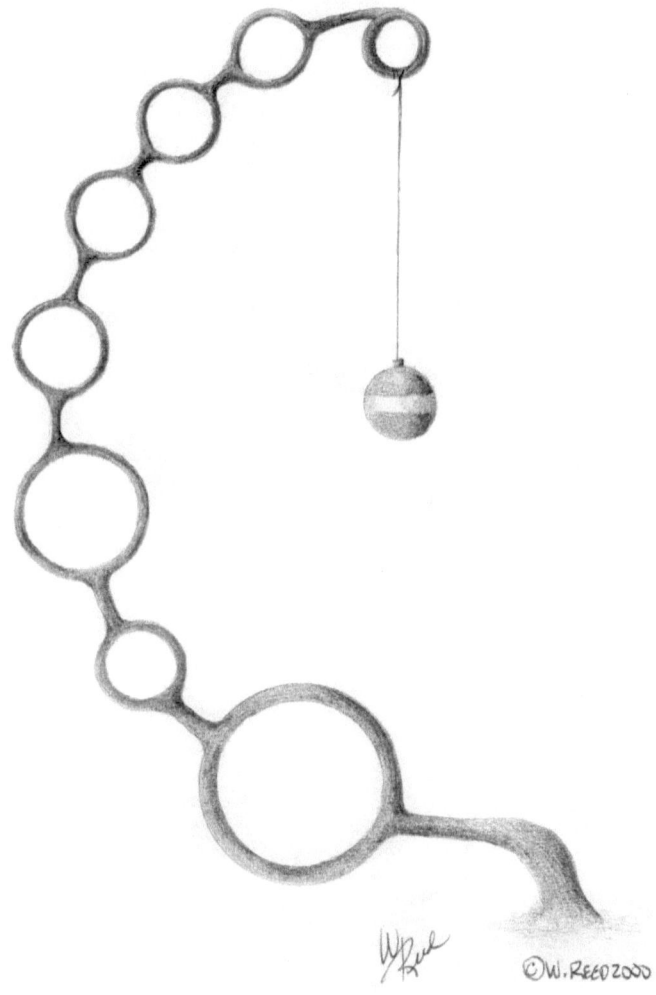

Christmas Card 2001

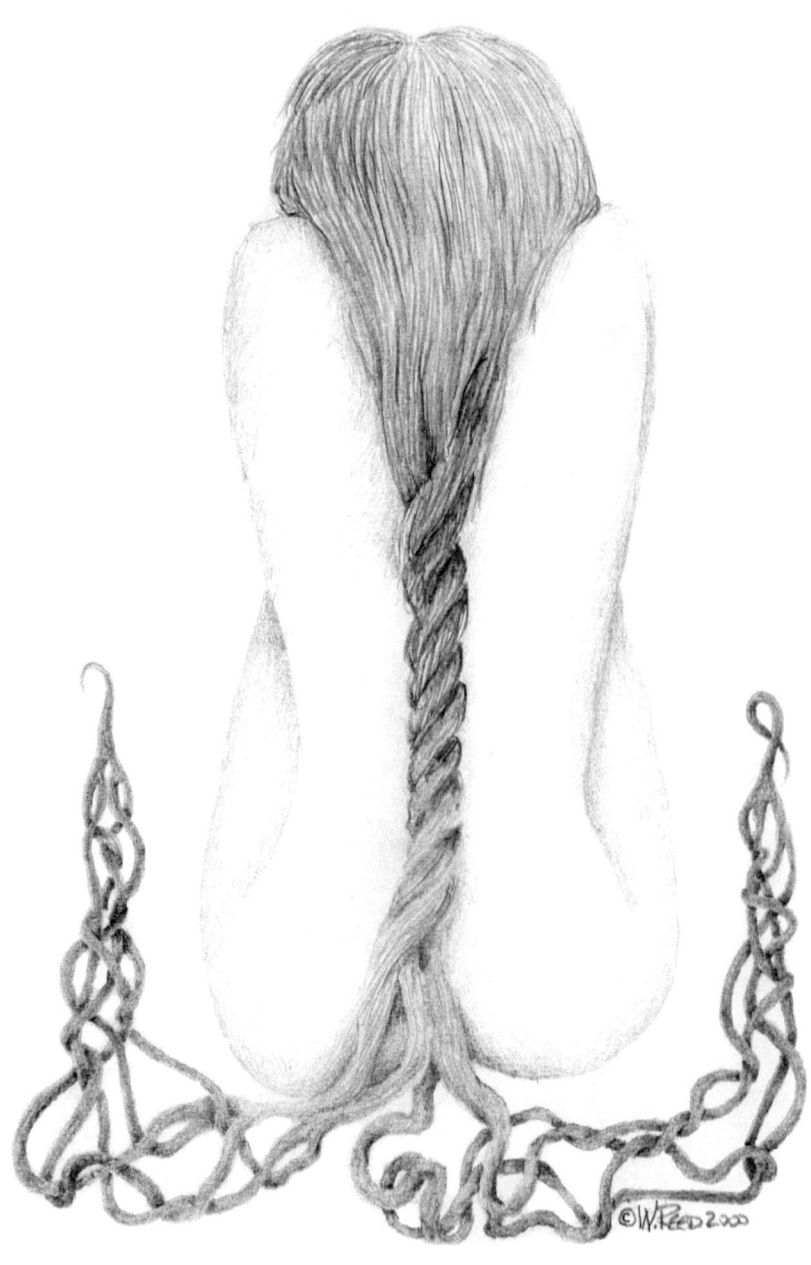

Unusual Hair Day

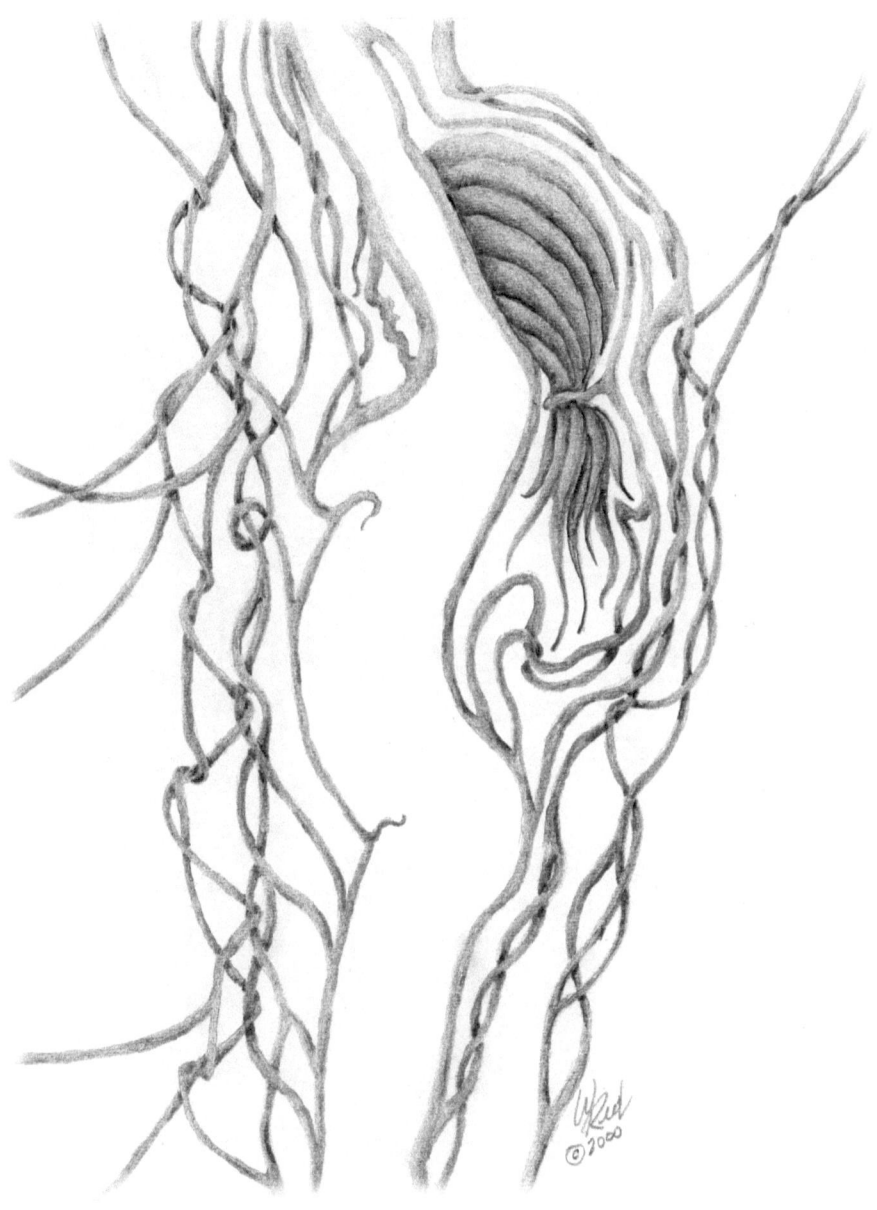

Growing

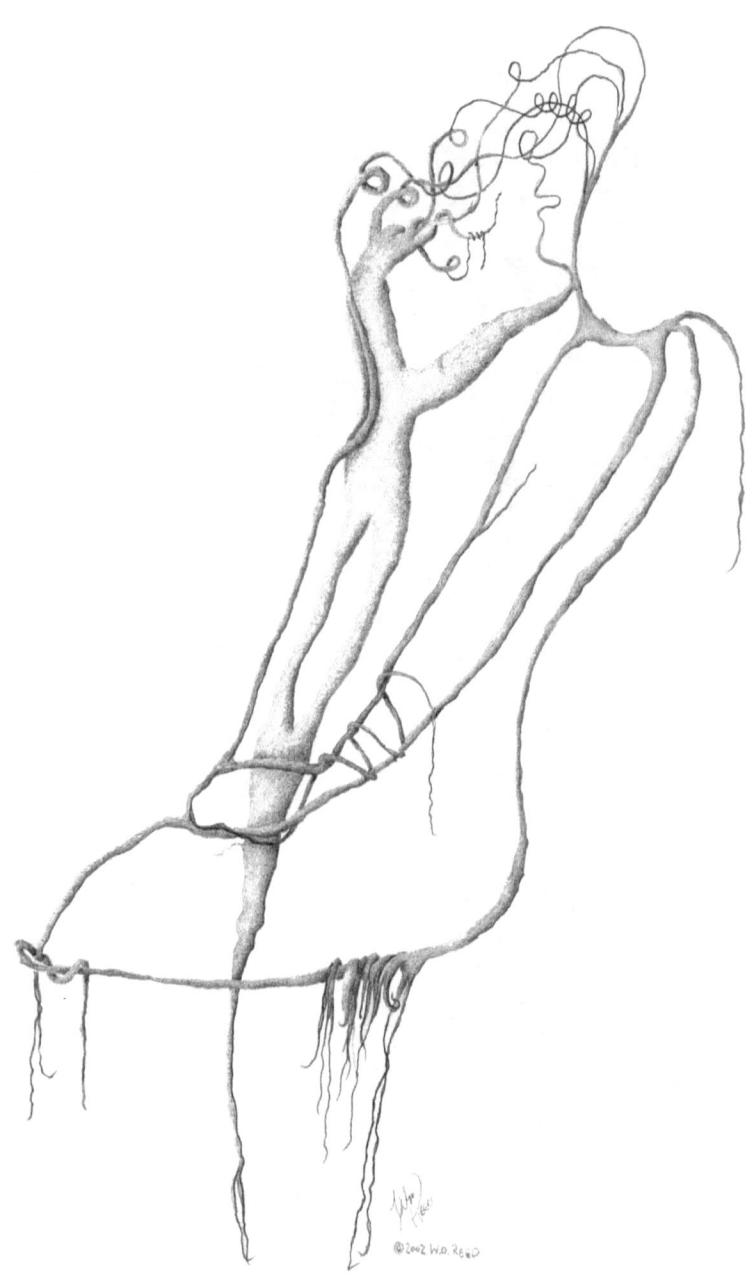

Retreating

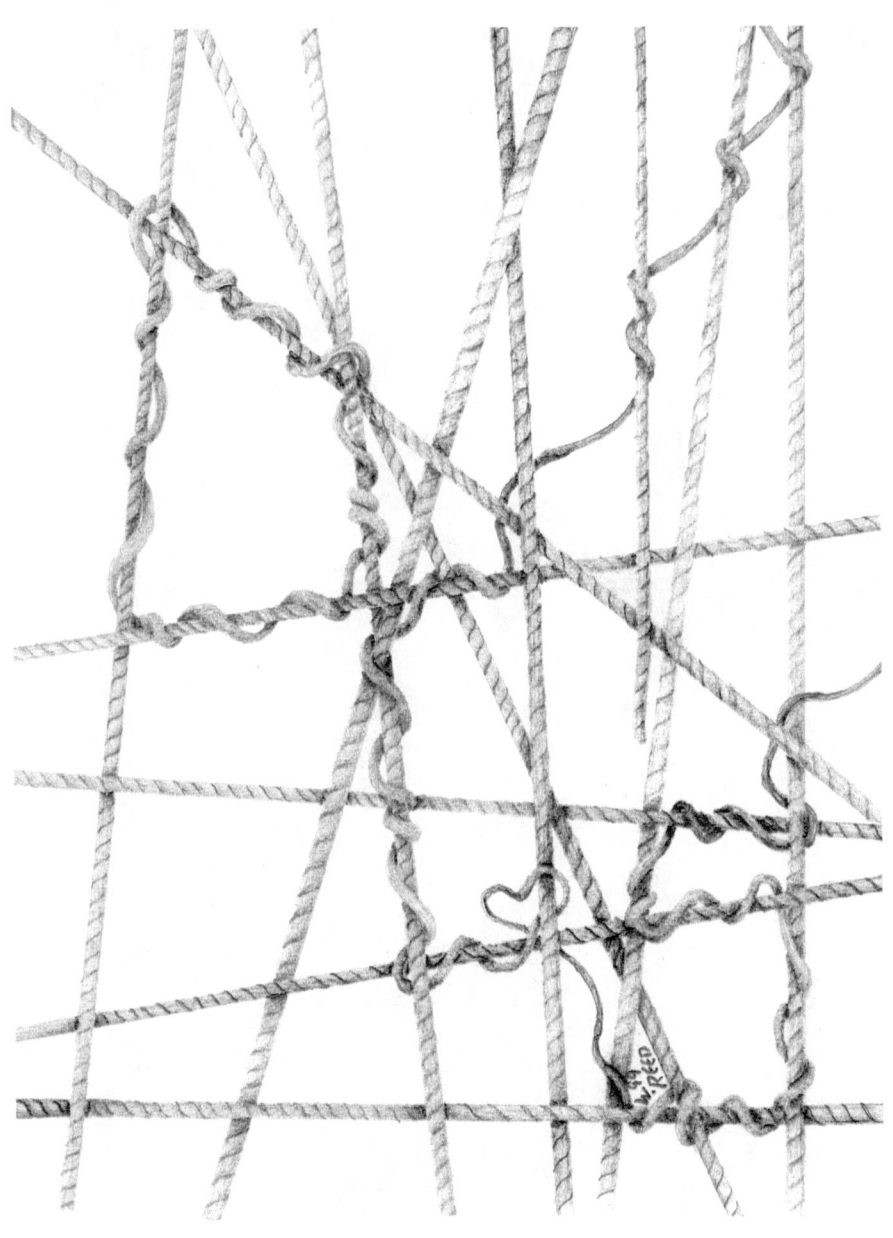

Love Weave

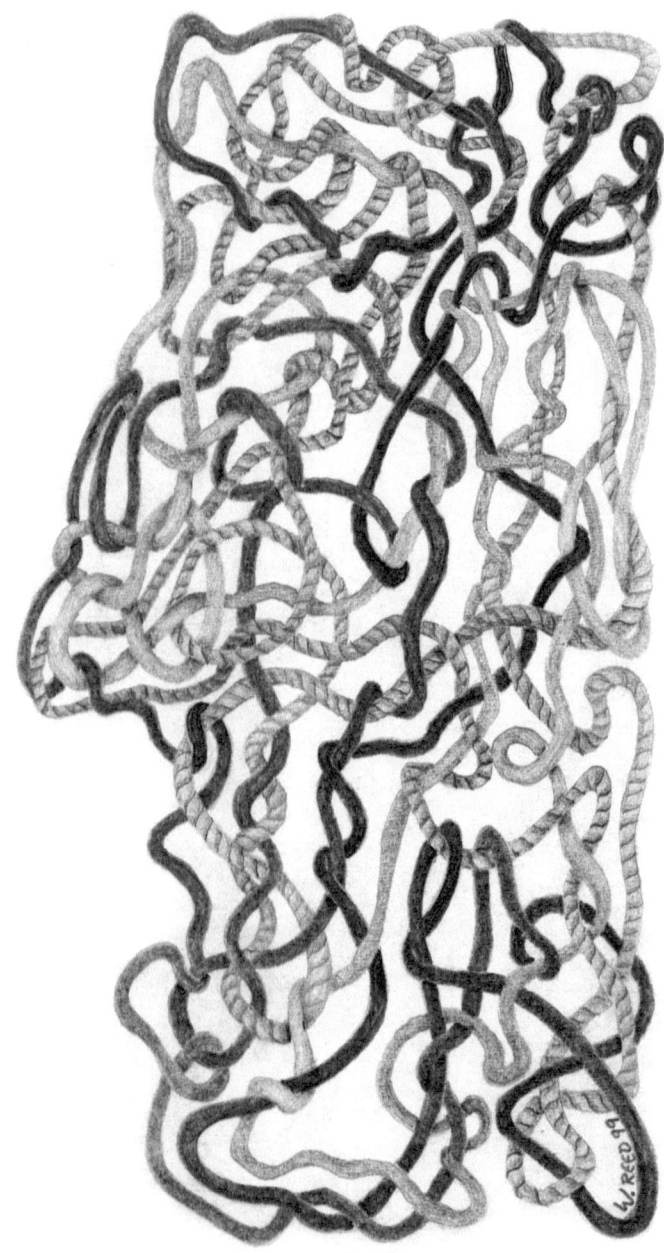

Face

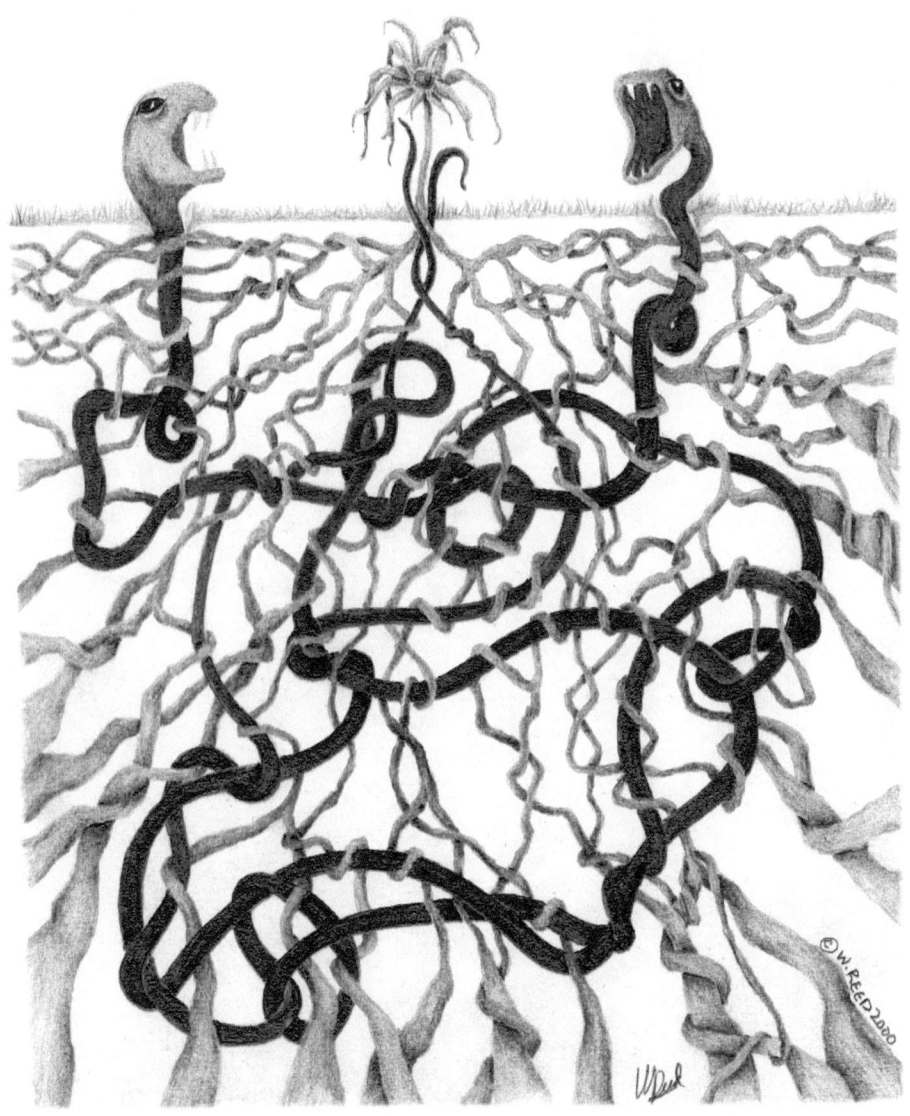

Brothers

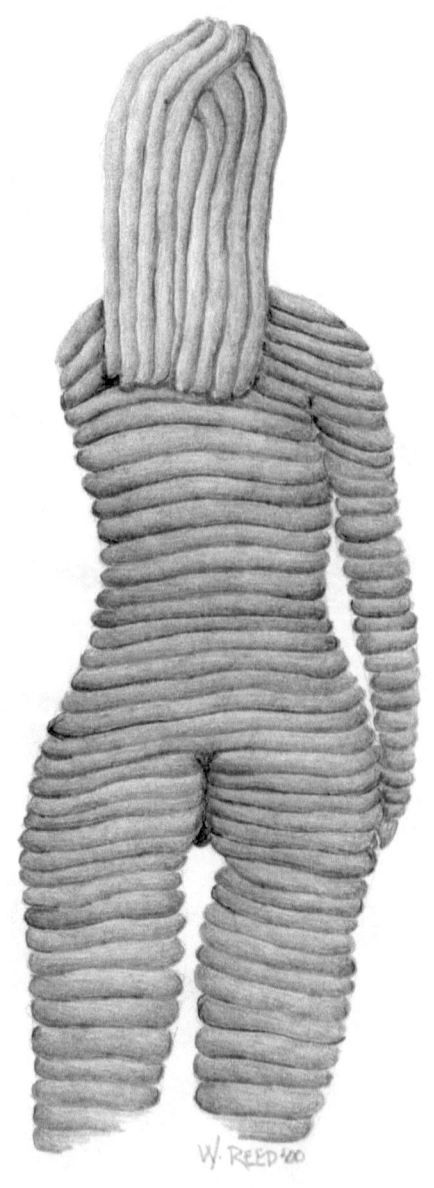

Gumbys' Mom

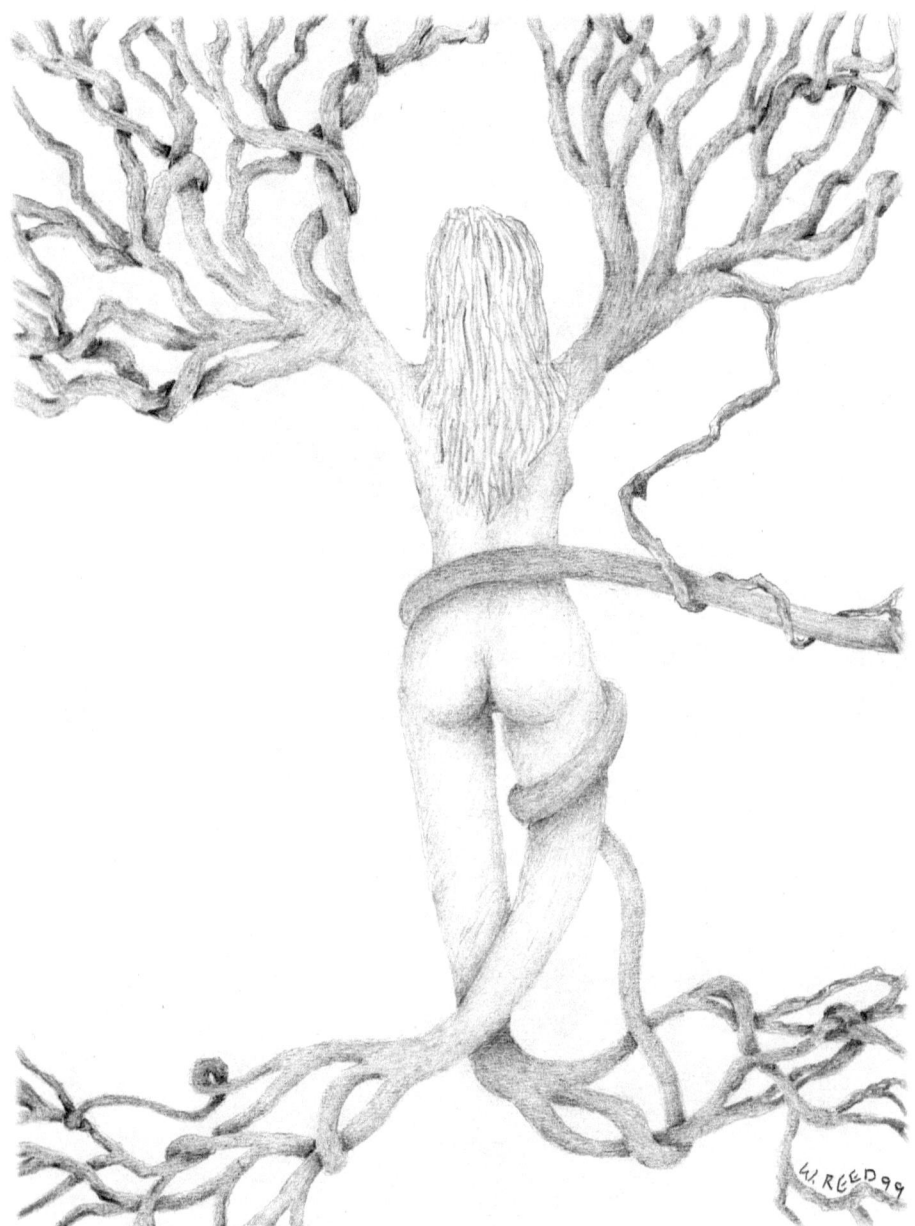

Sarah

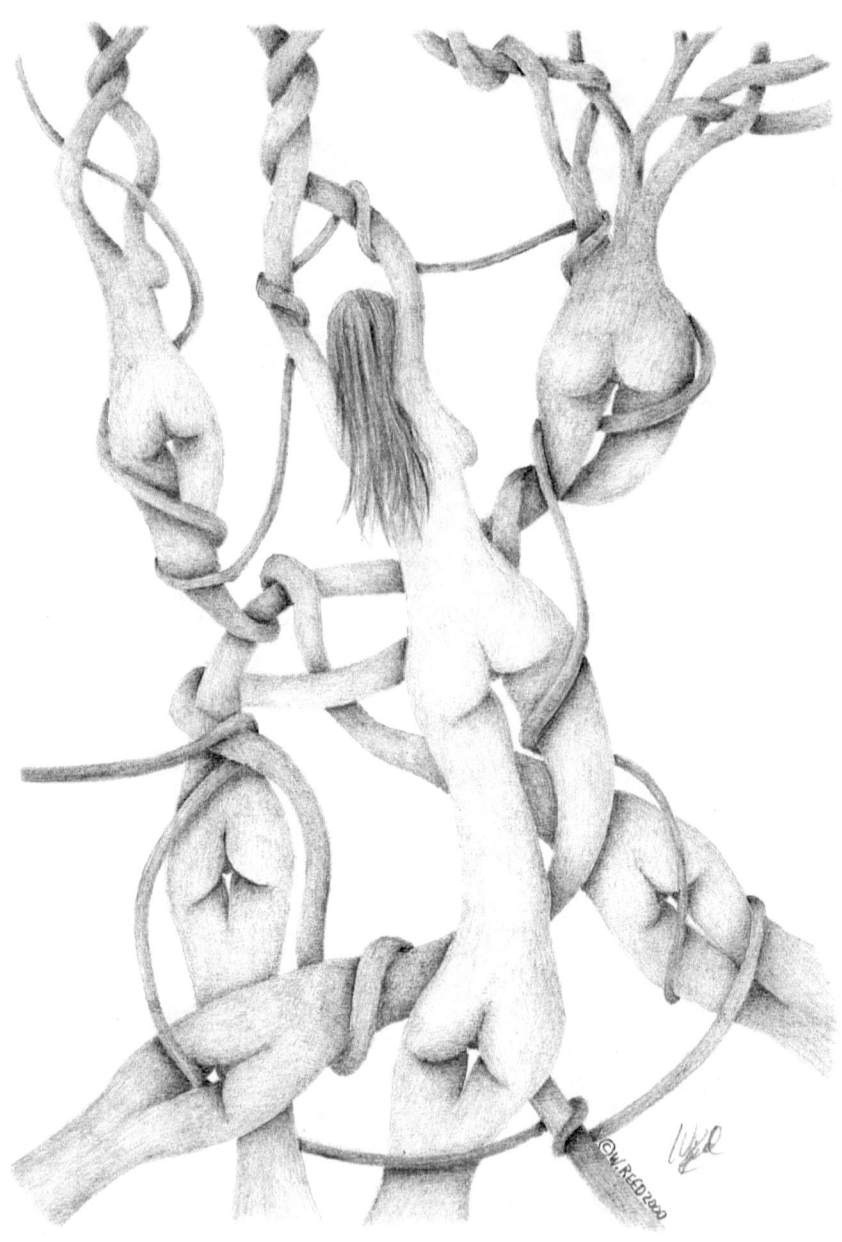

The Struggle

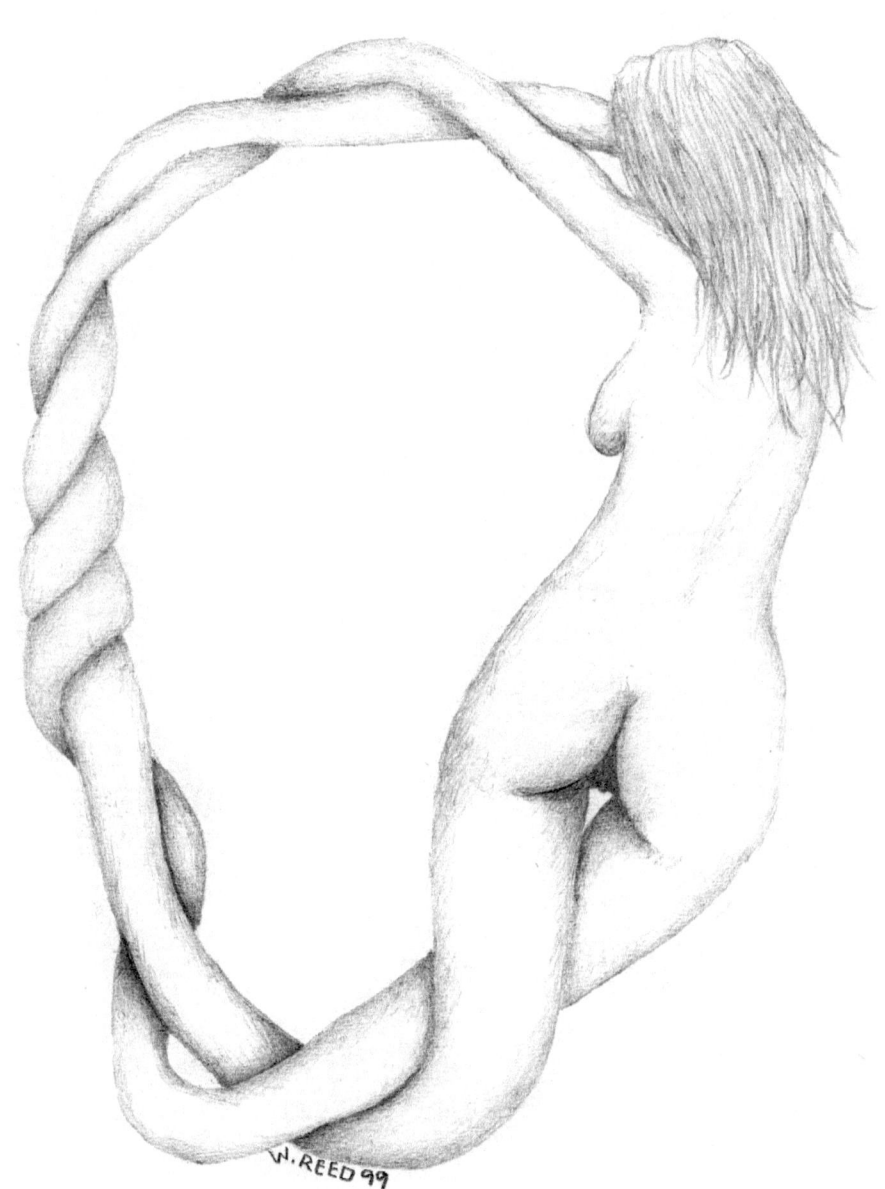

Ring Her

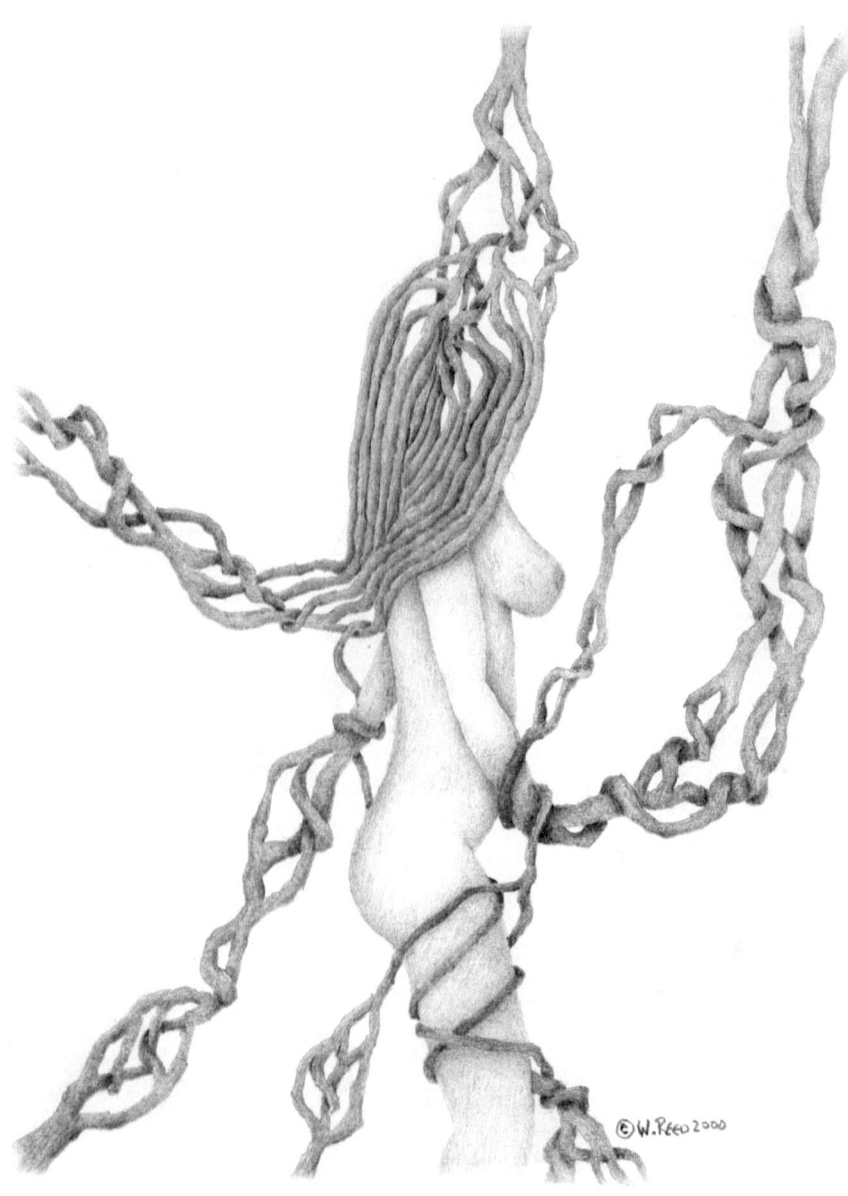

Laura

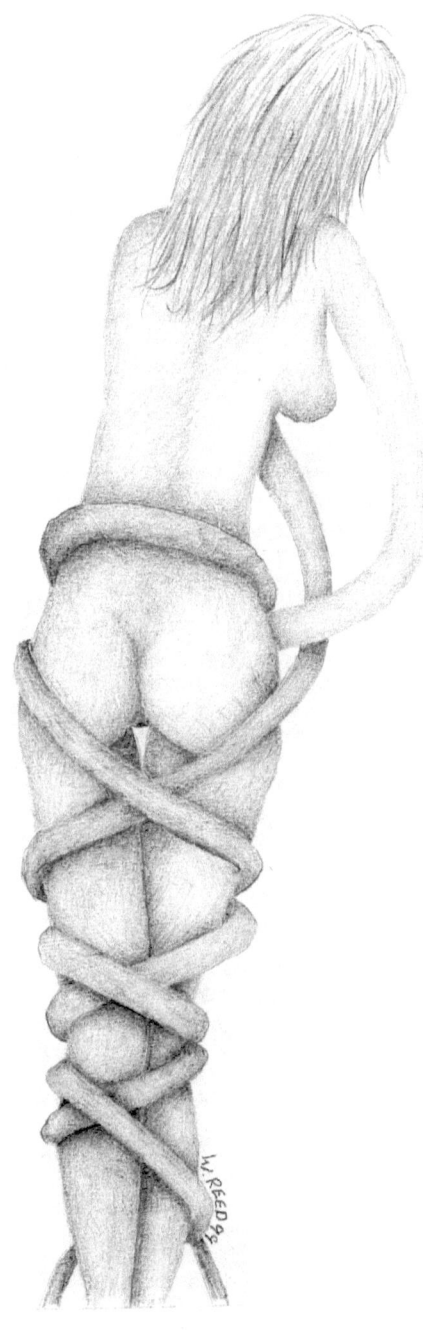

Bound

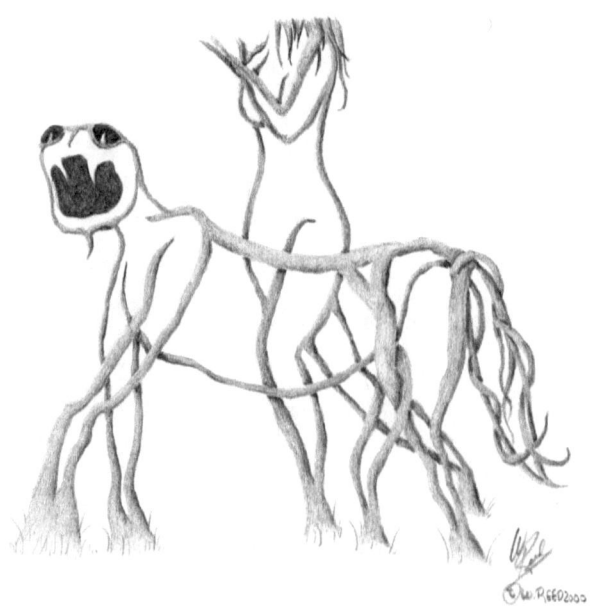

Fury

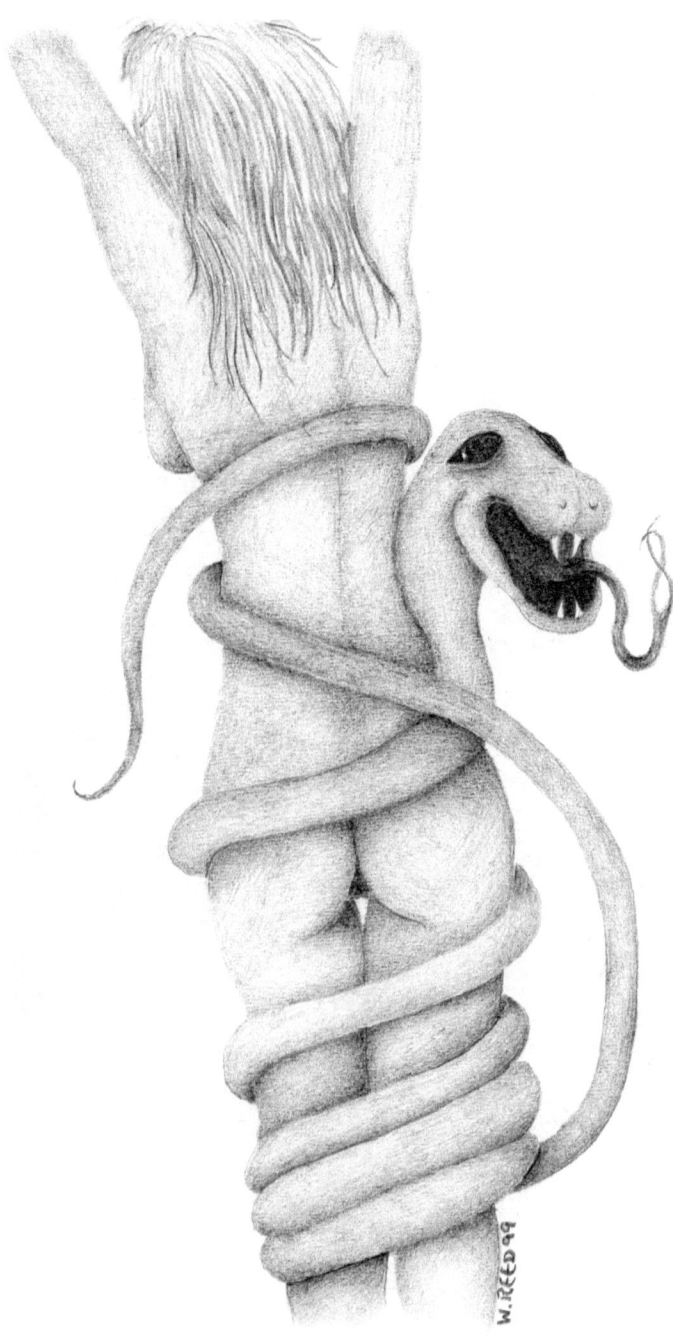

Charmed

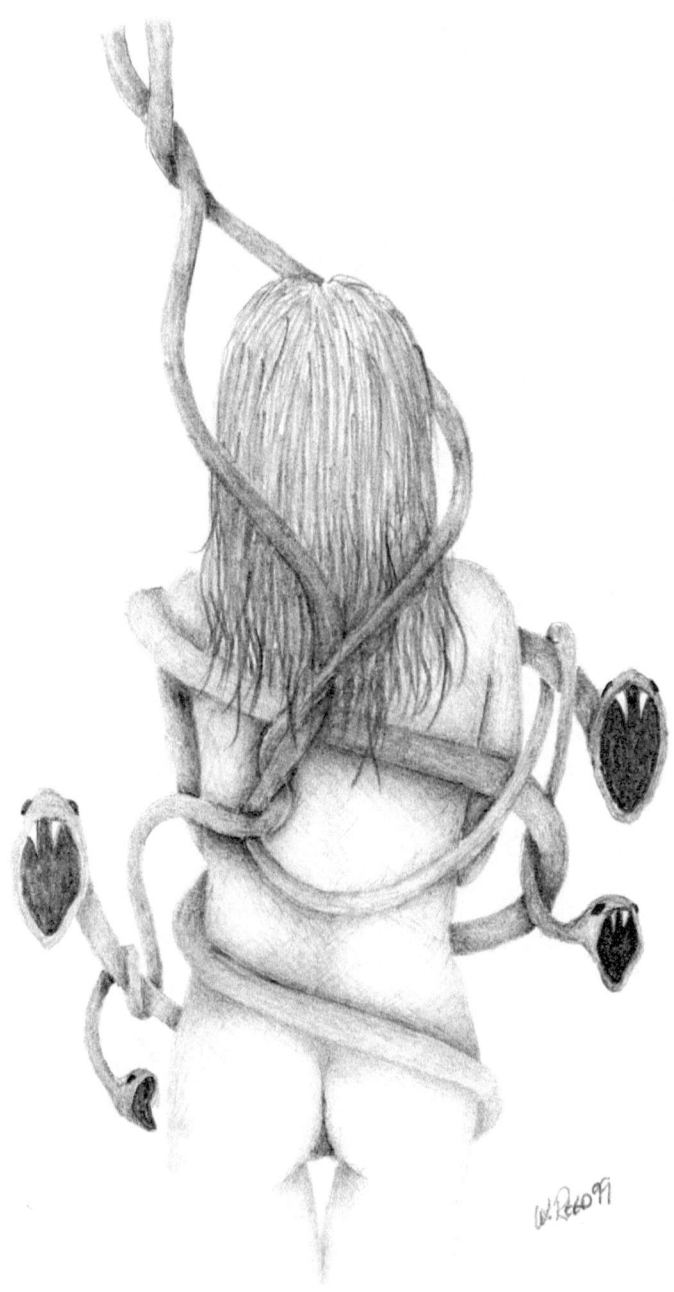

Snake Charmed

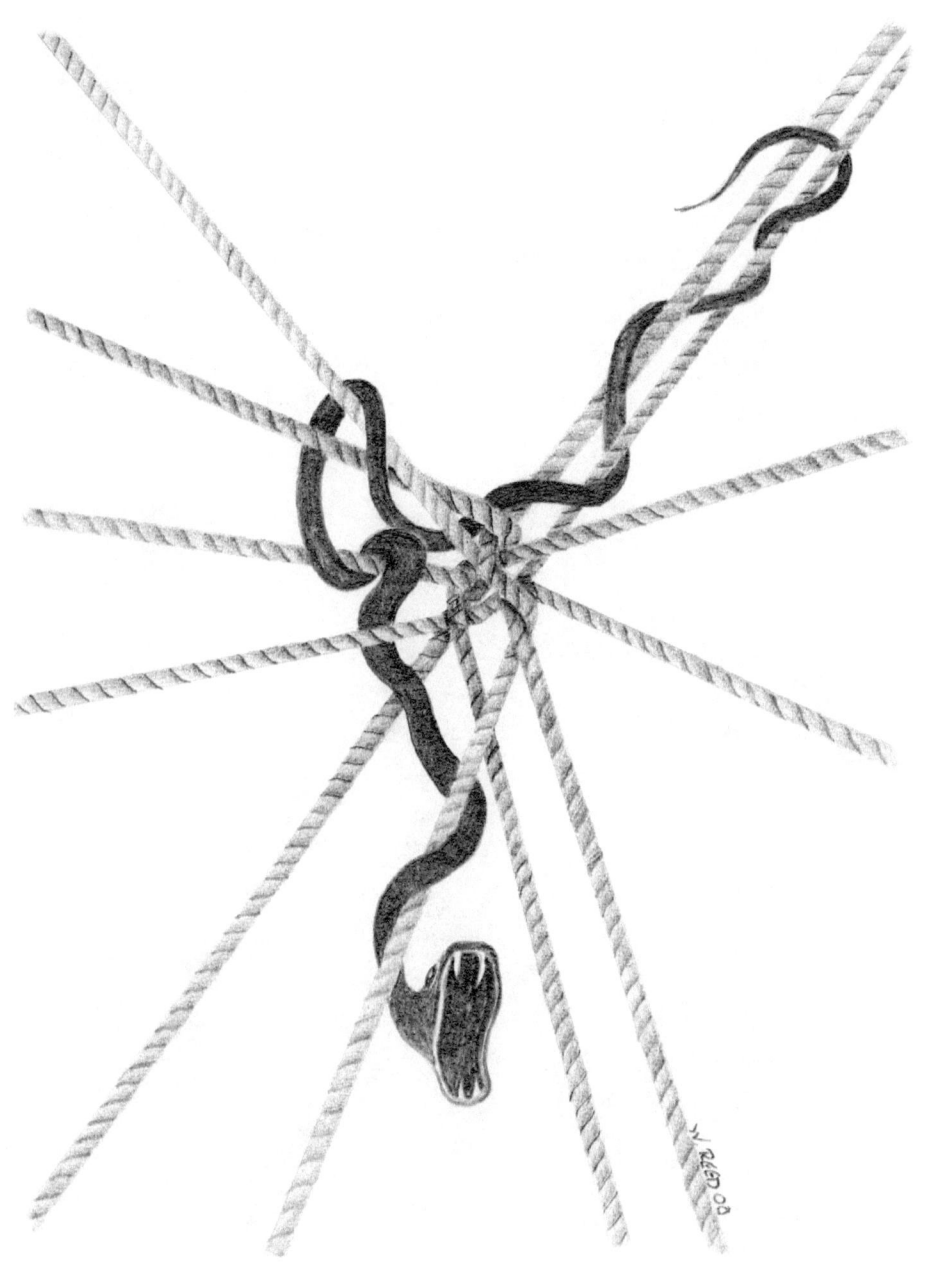

Nexus

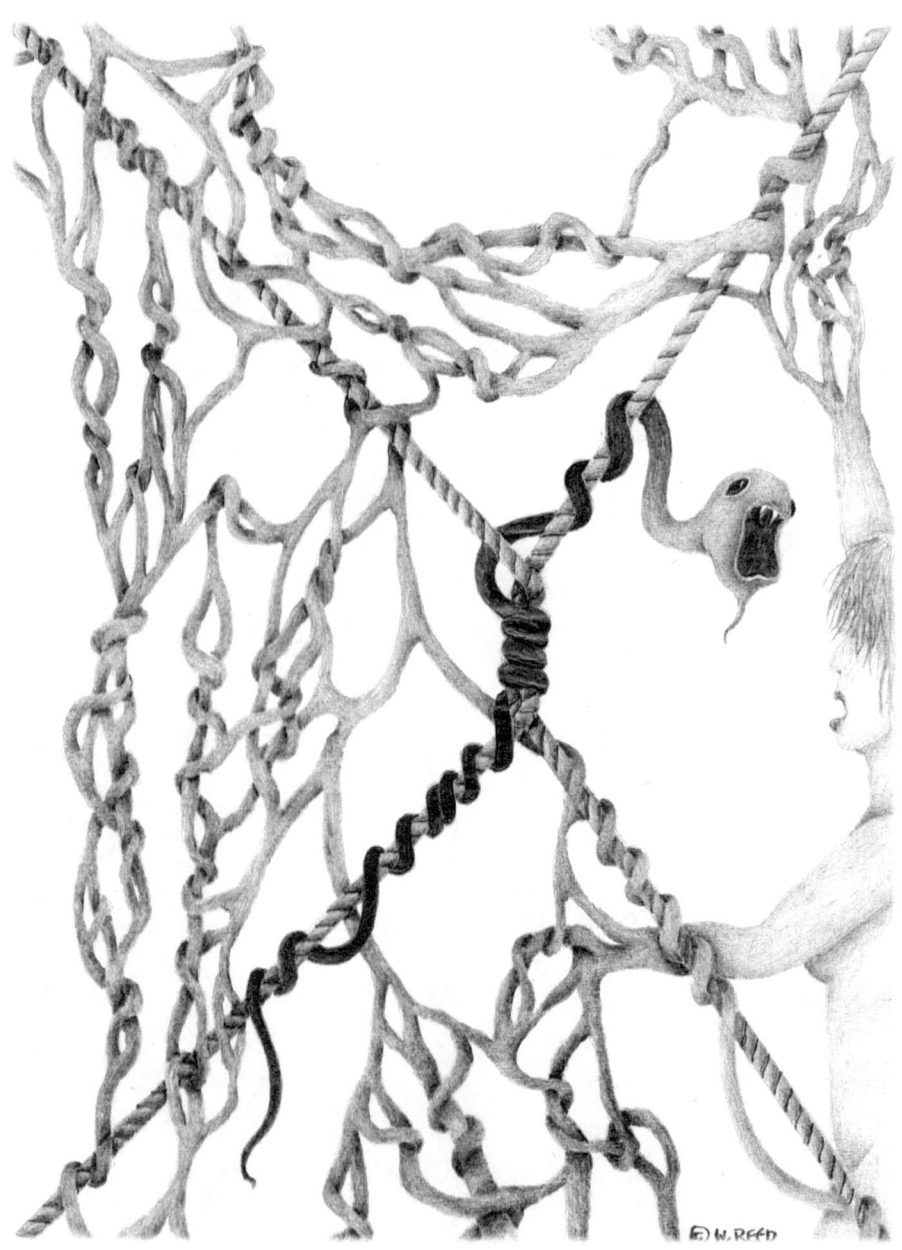

Eves' Dilema

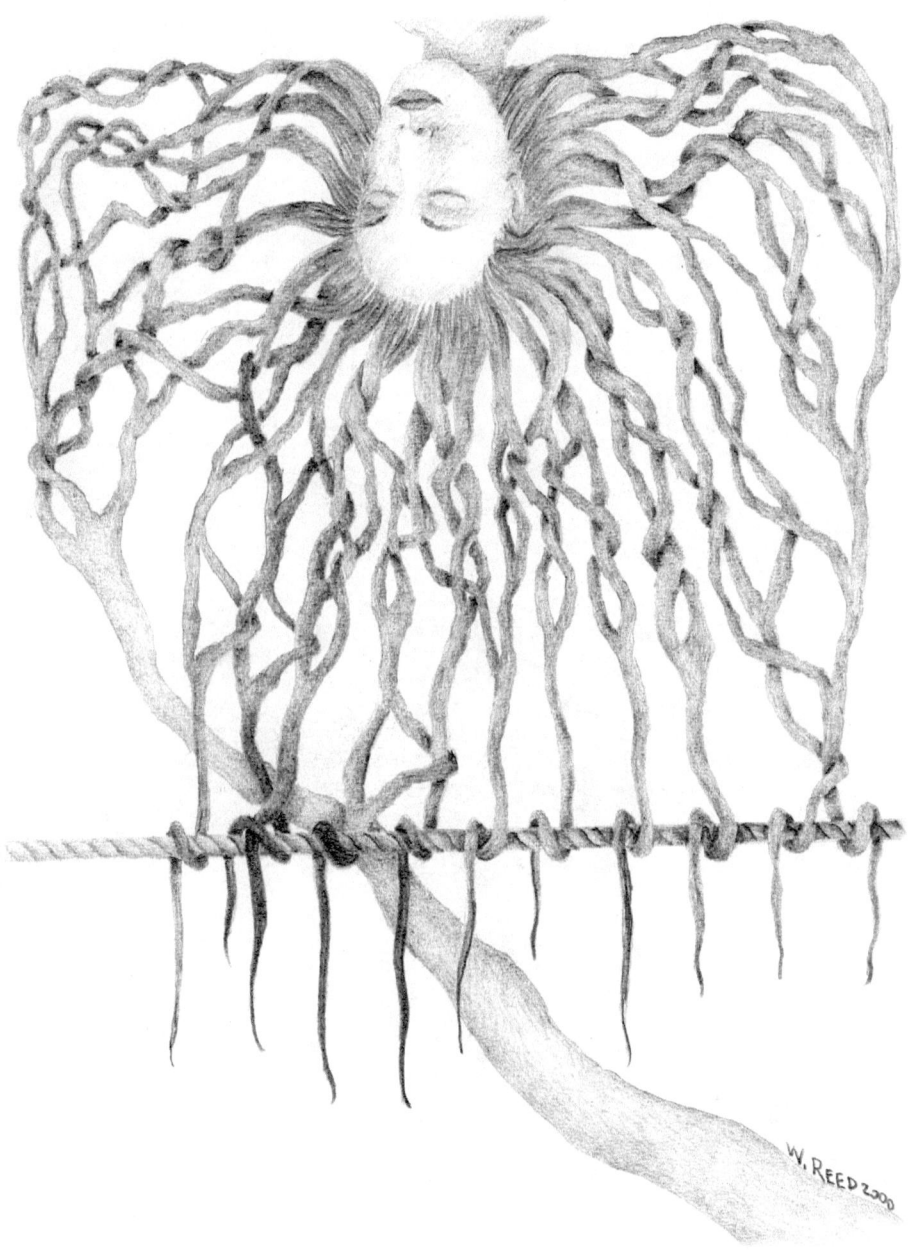

Relaxing

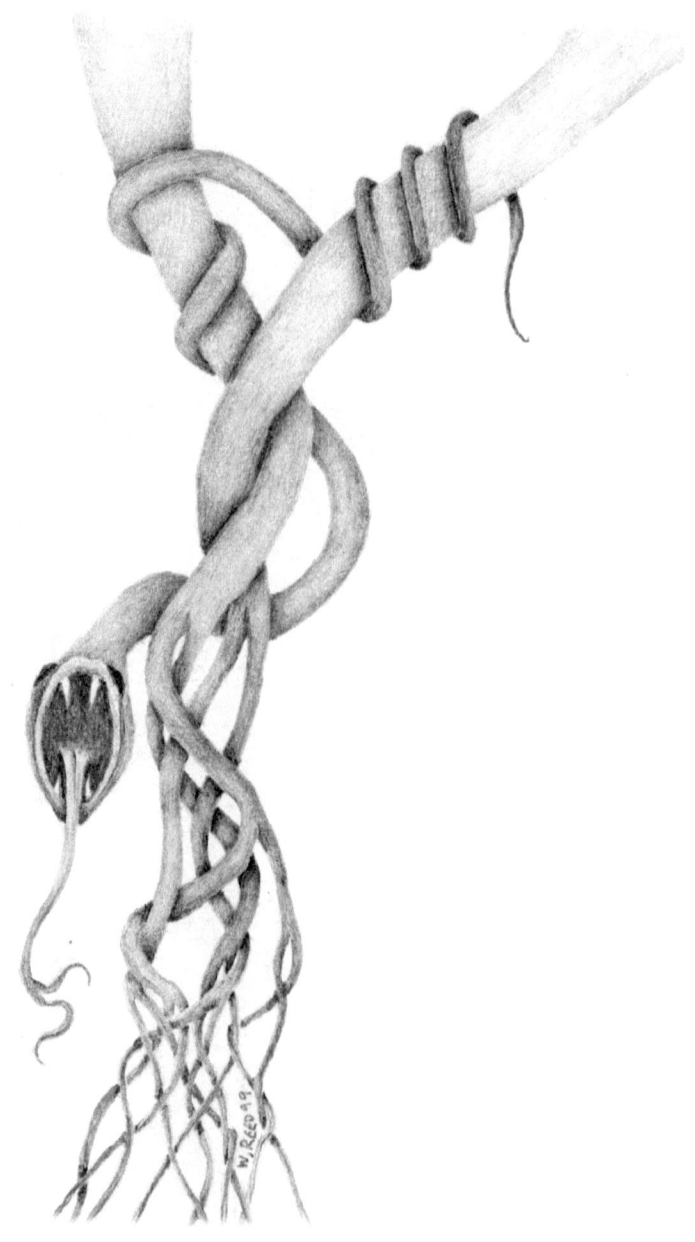

Decending

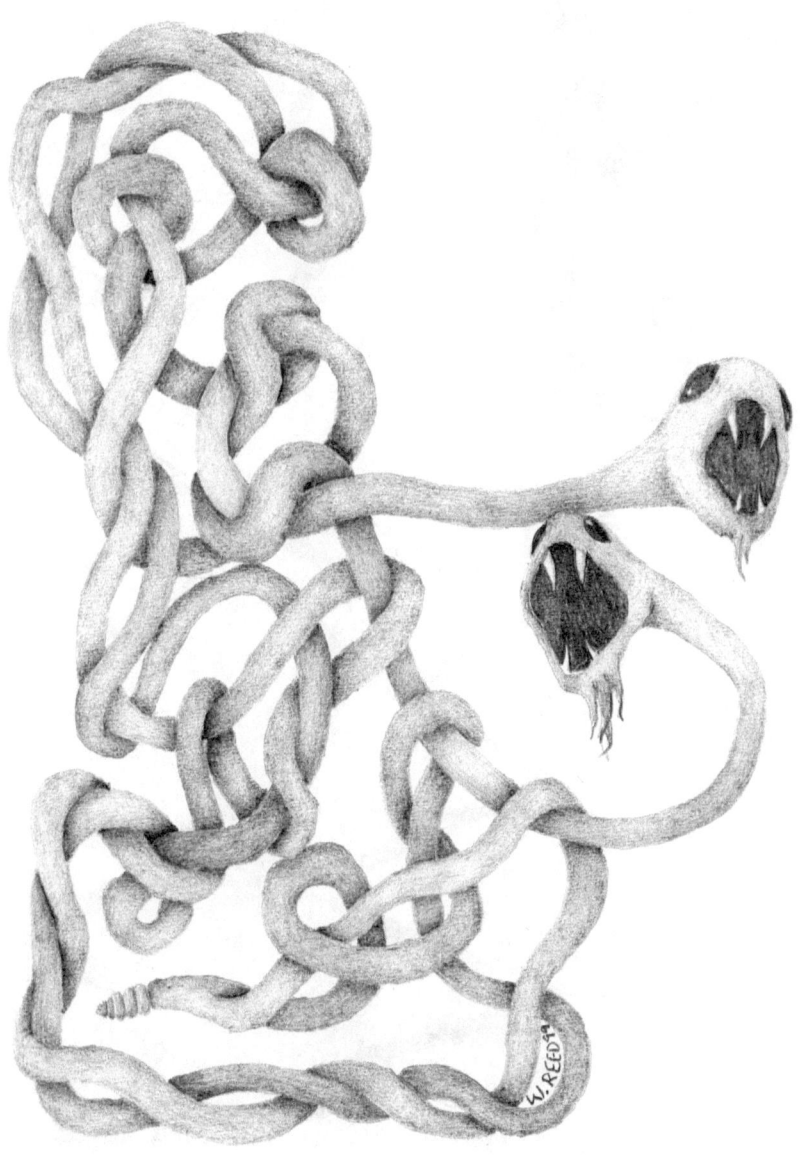

Siamese Snakes

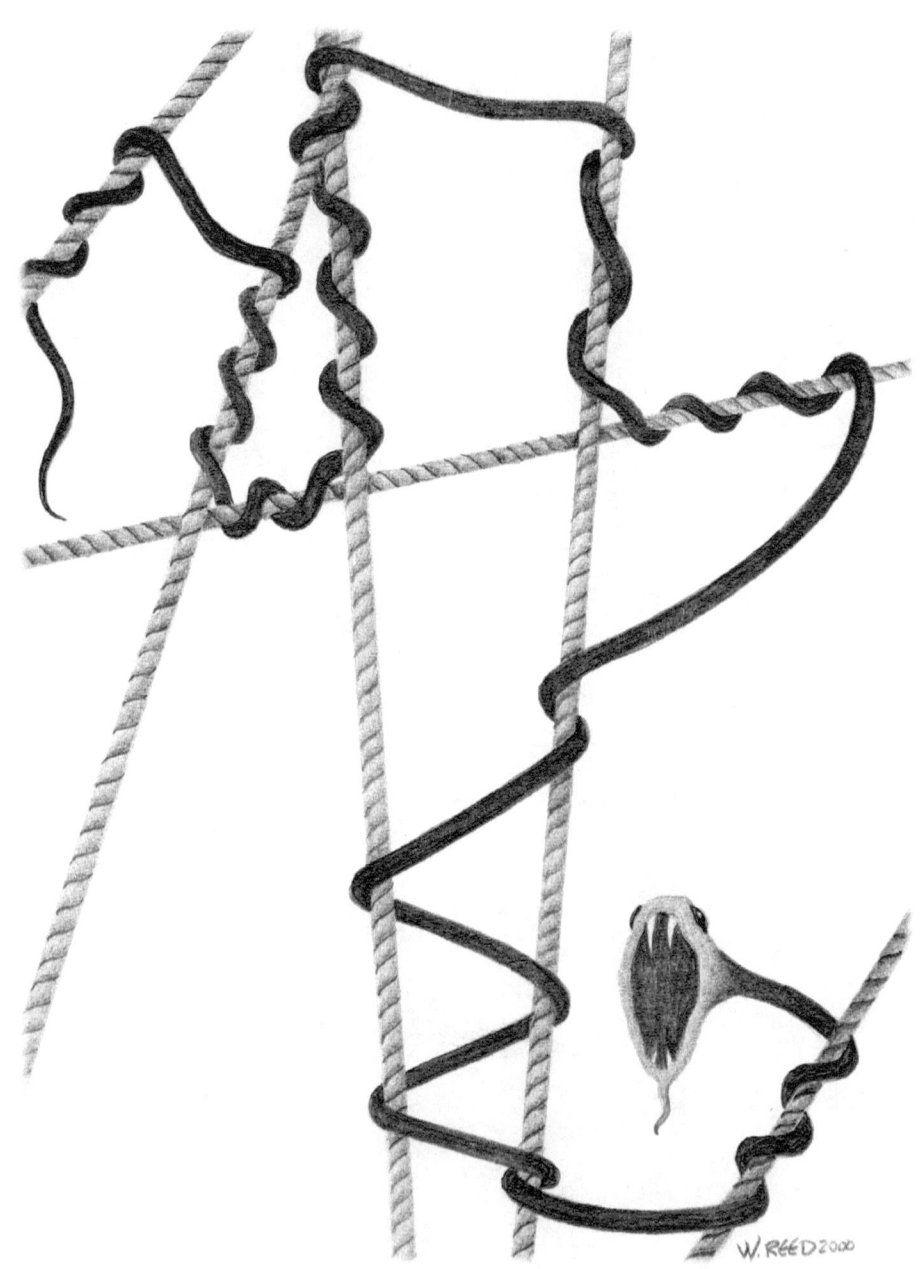

Entwined

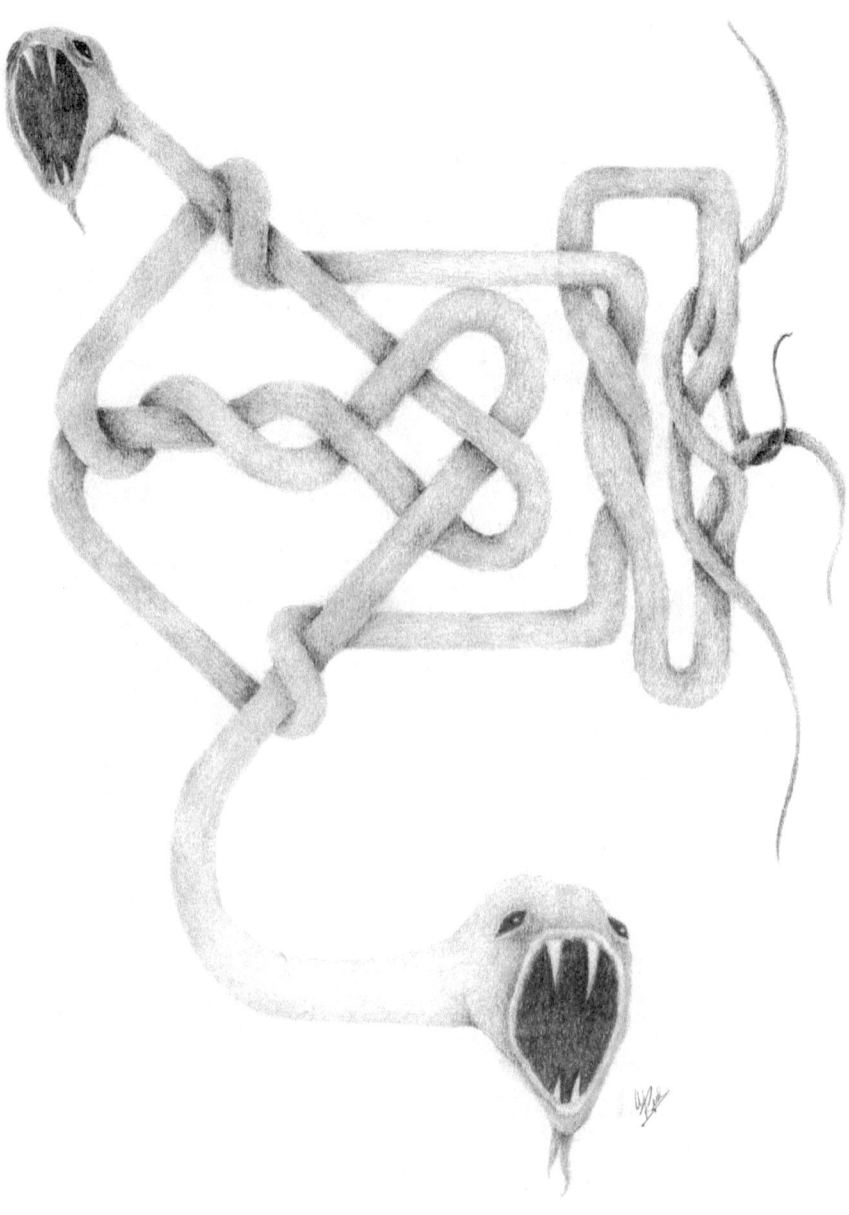

Embrace

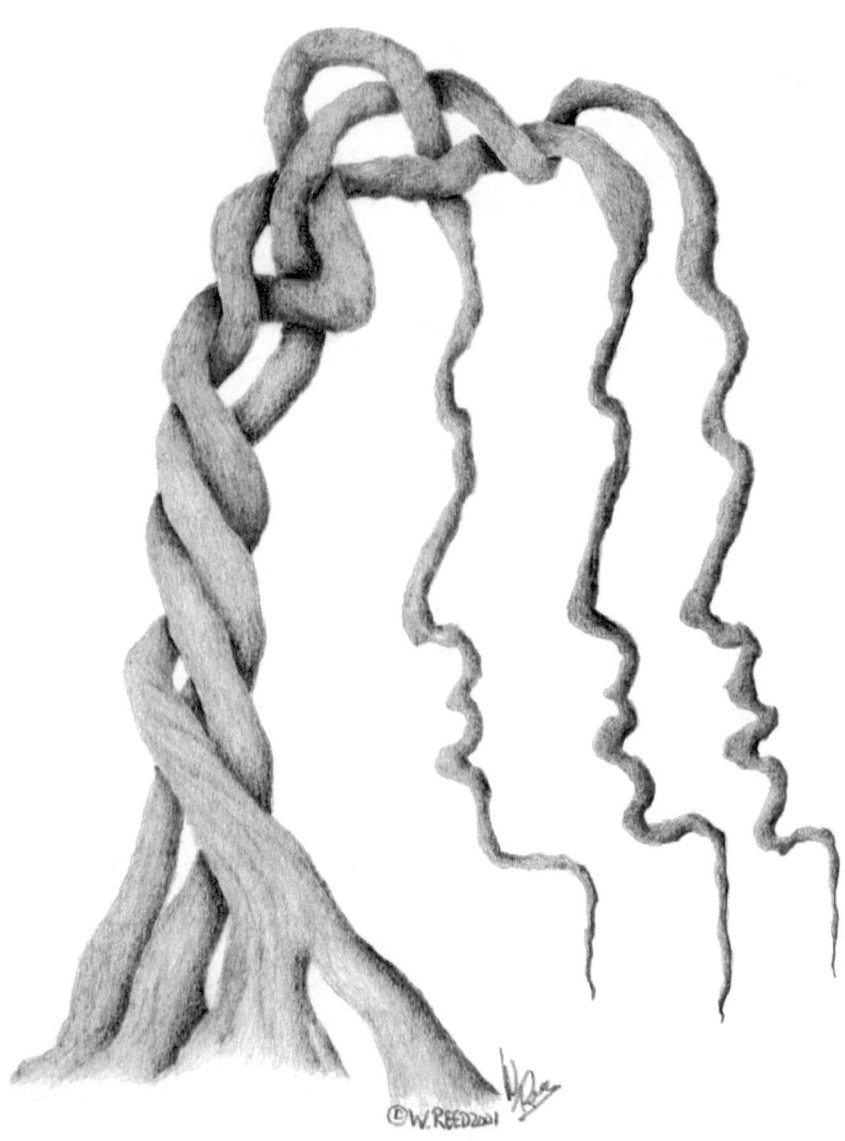

©W.REED2001

Tre Brothers

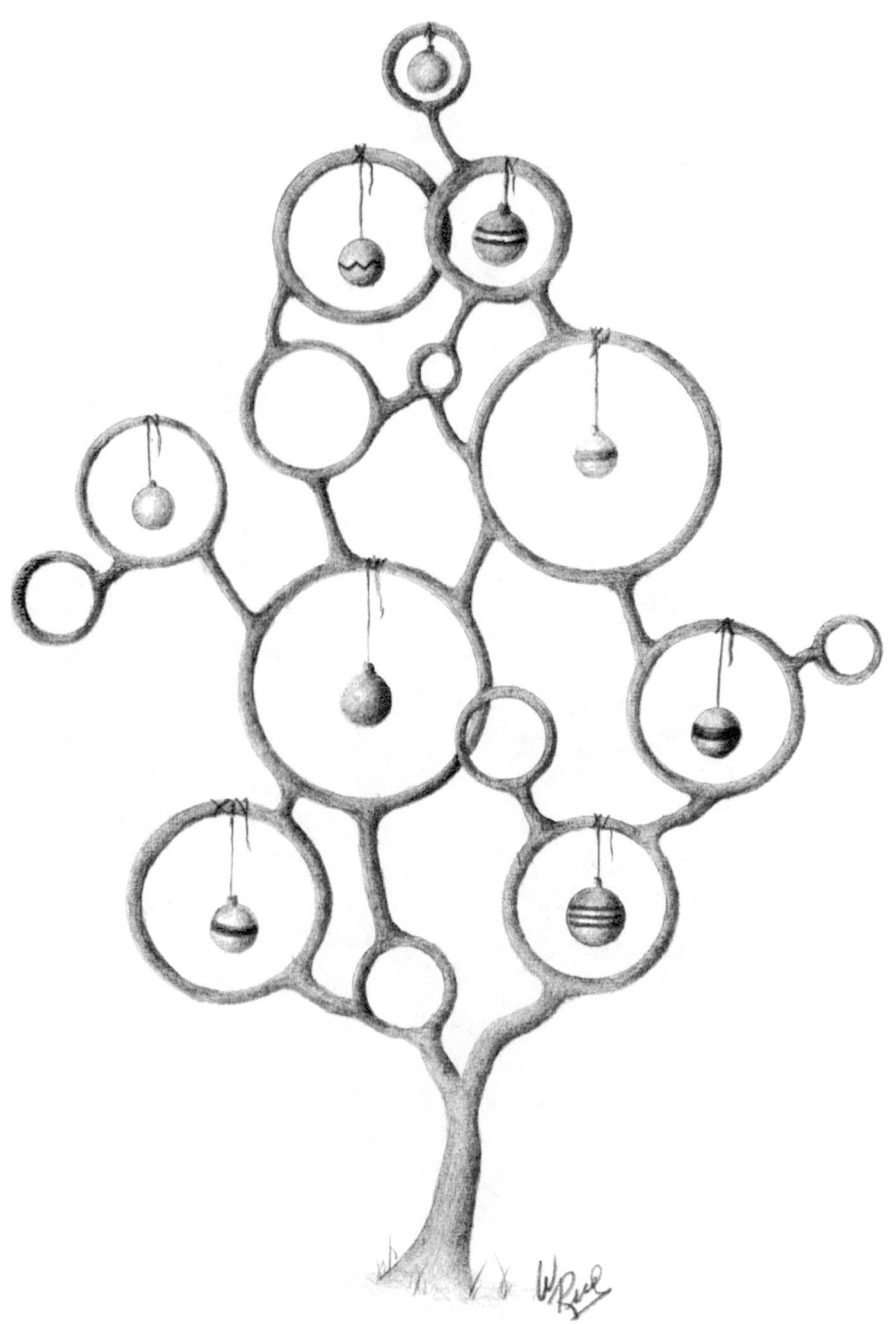

Chritstmas Card 2001

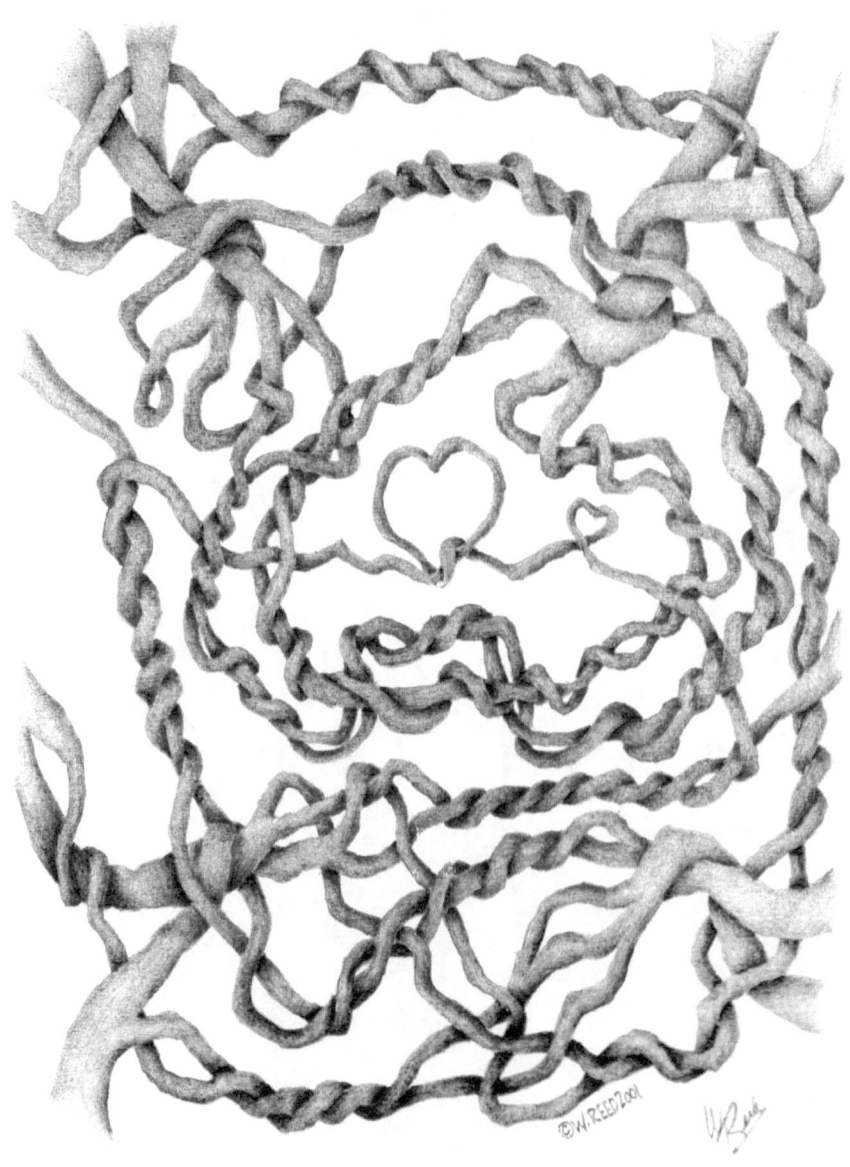

Heart

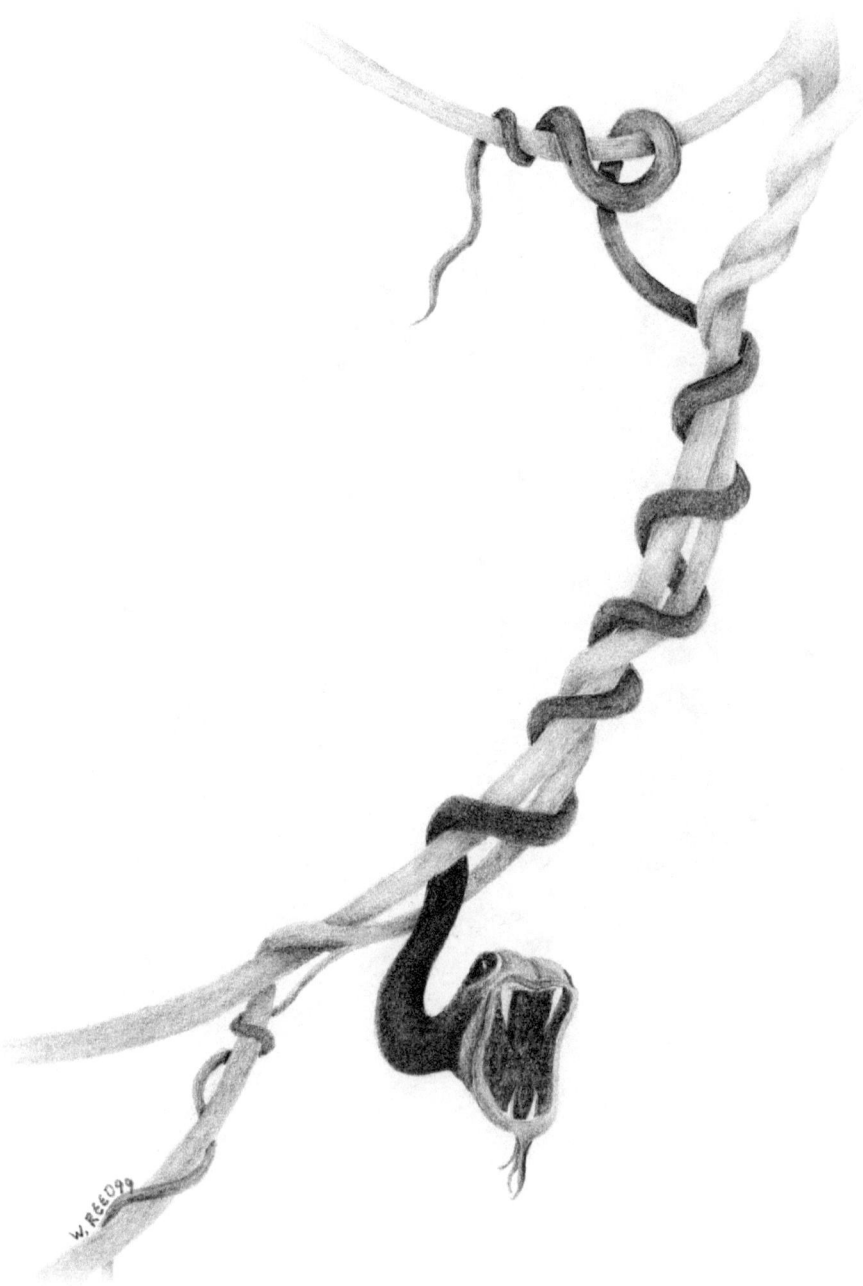

Hangtime

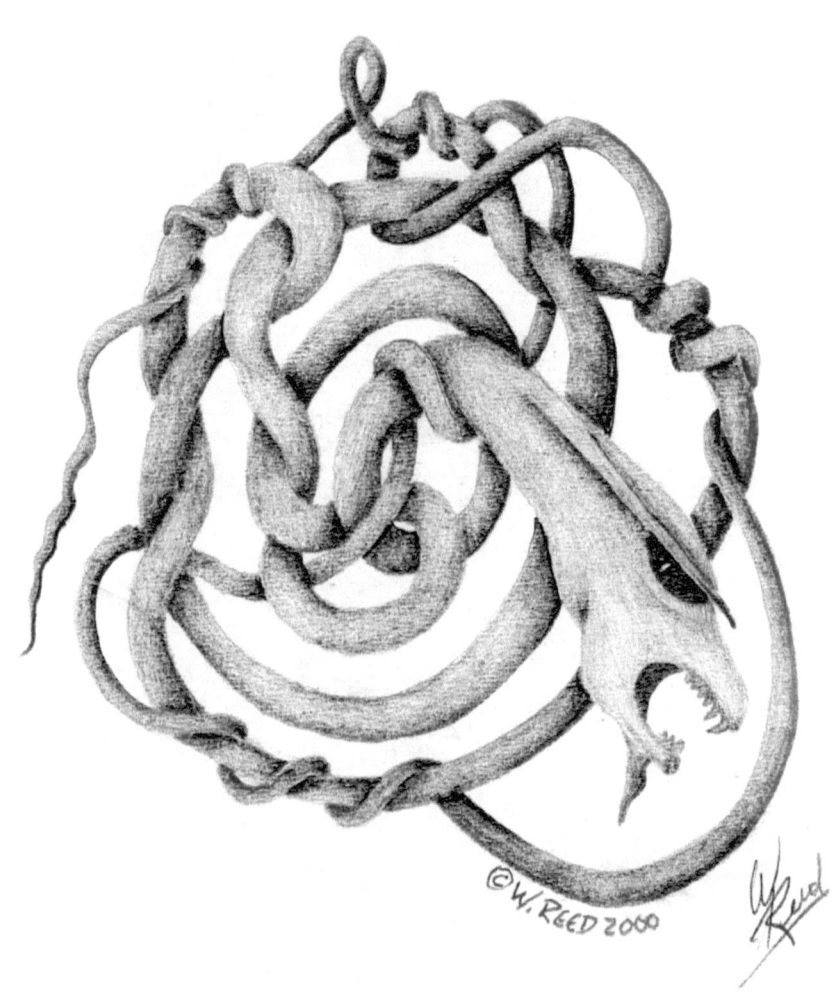

Serpentine Twist

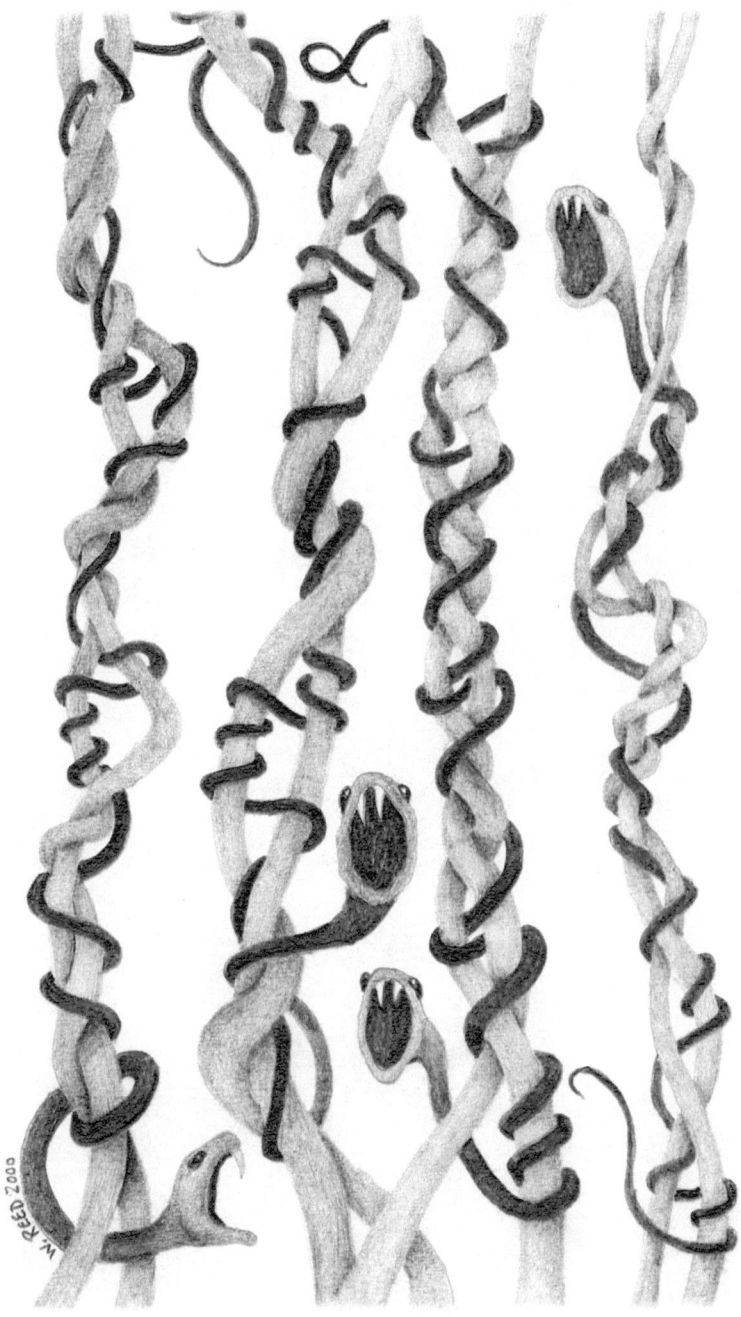

Brothers 4

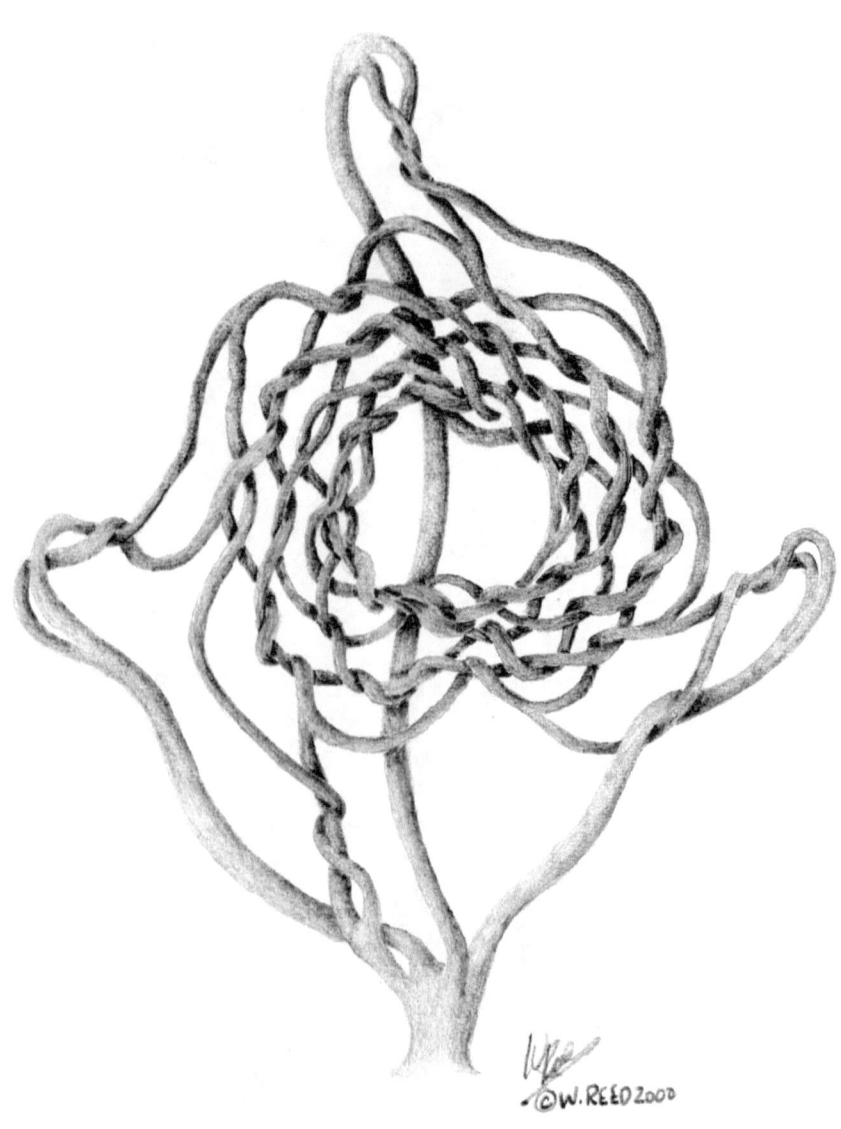

©W. REED 2000

What, me worry?

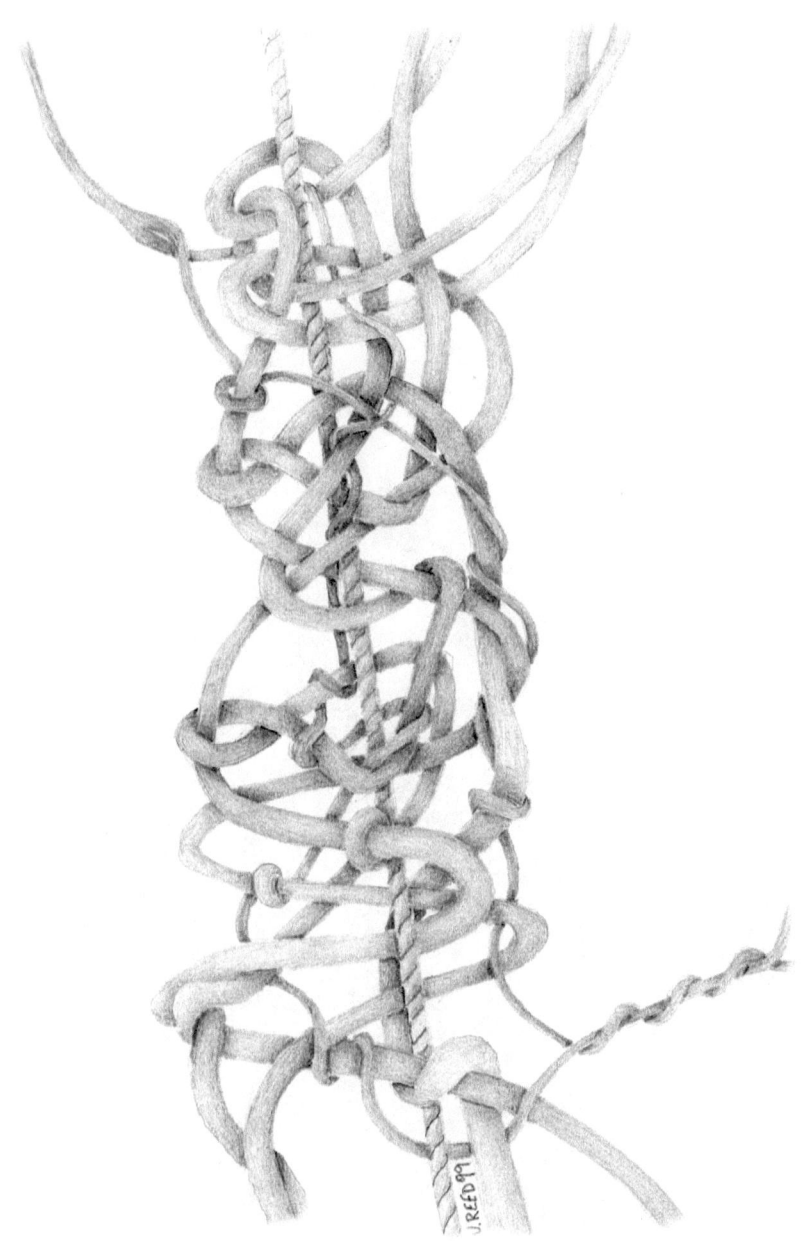

Gauntlet

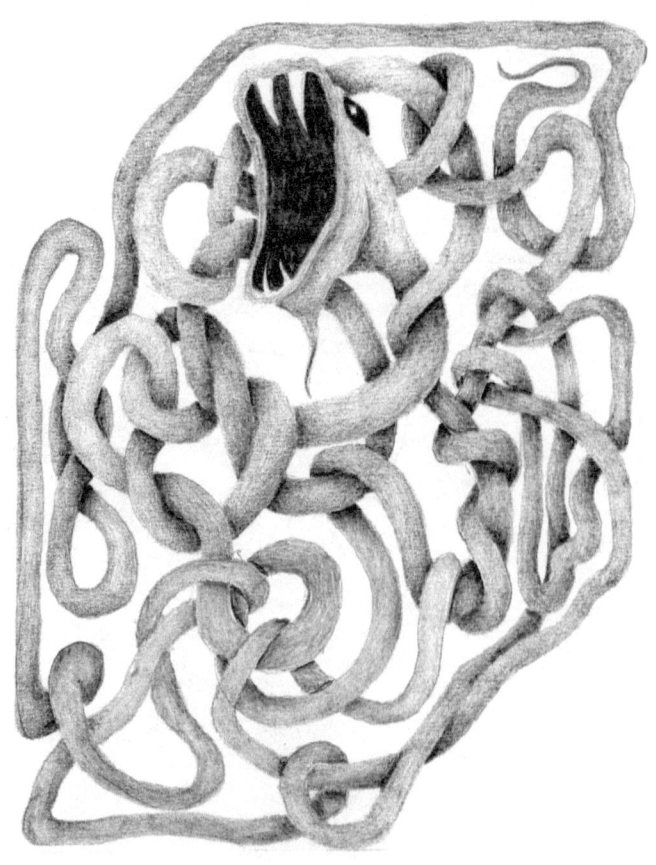

Inside the box

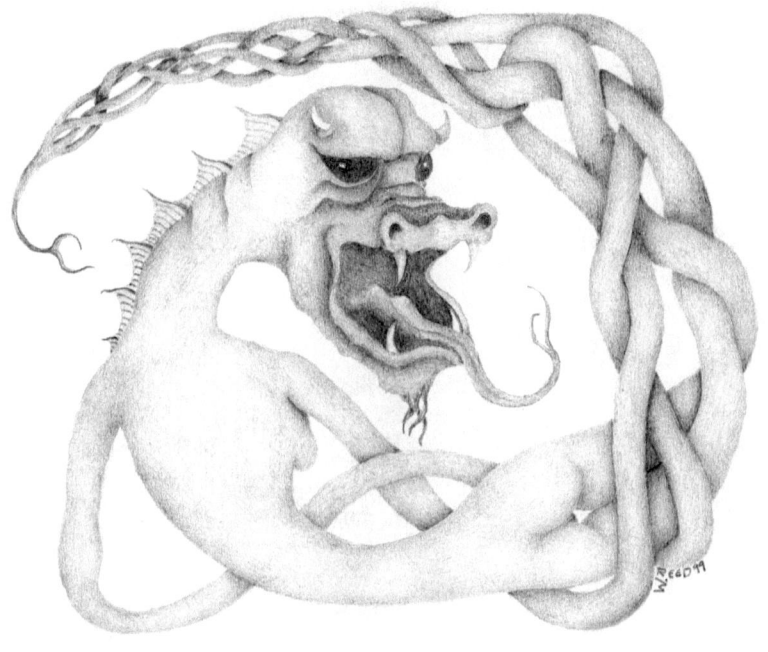

Dragon Lady

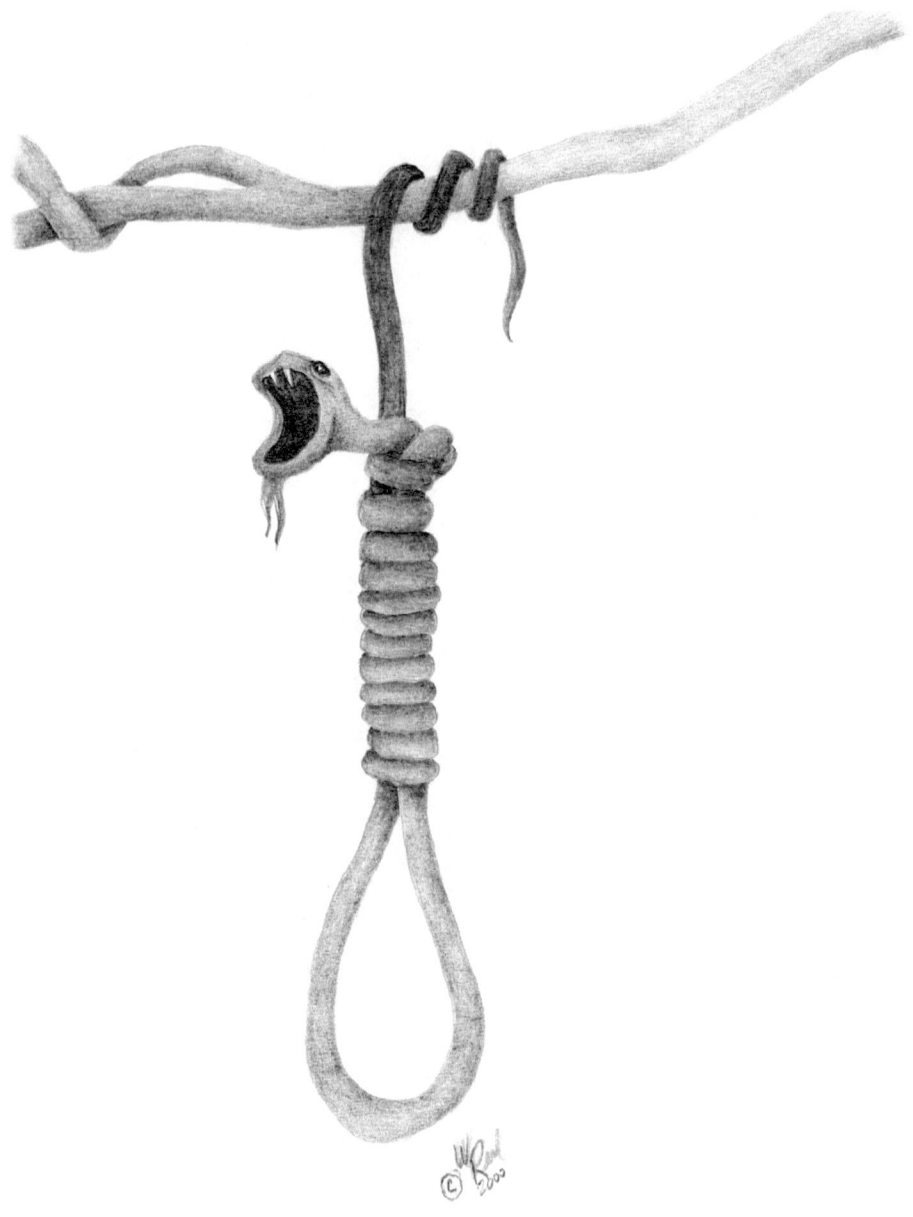

Noosnake

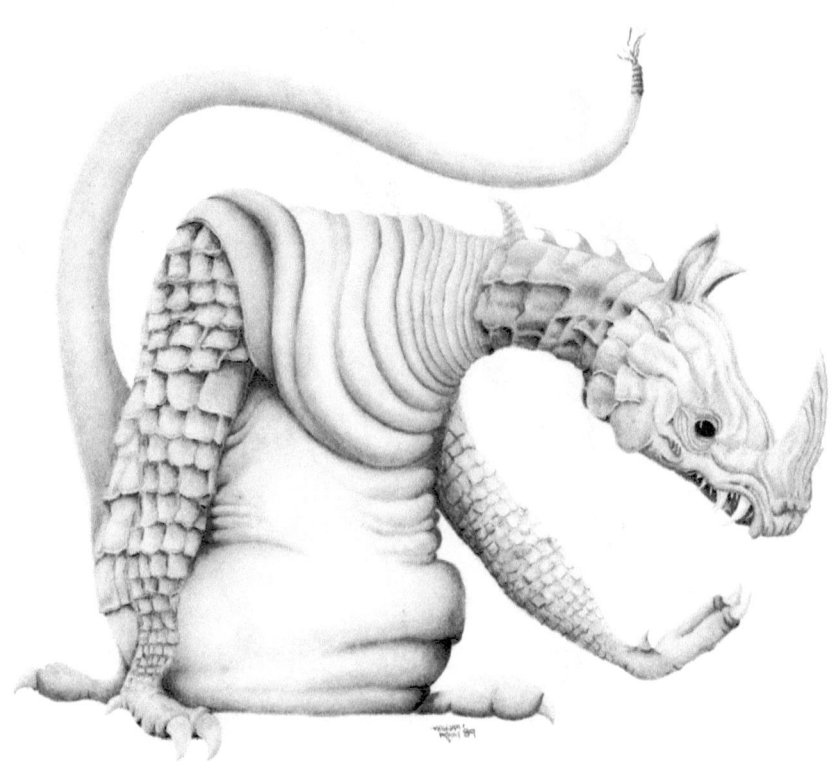

Discovering

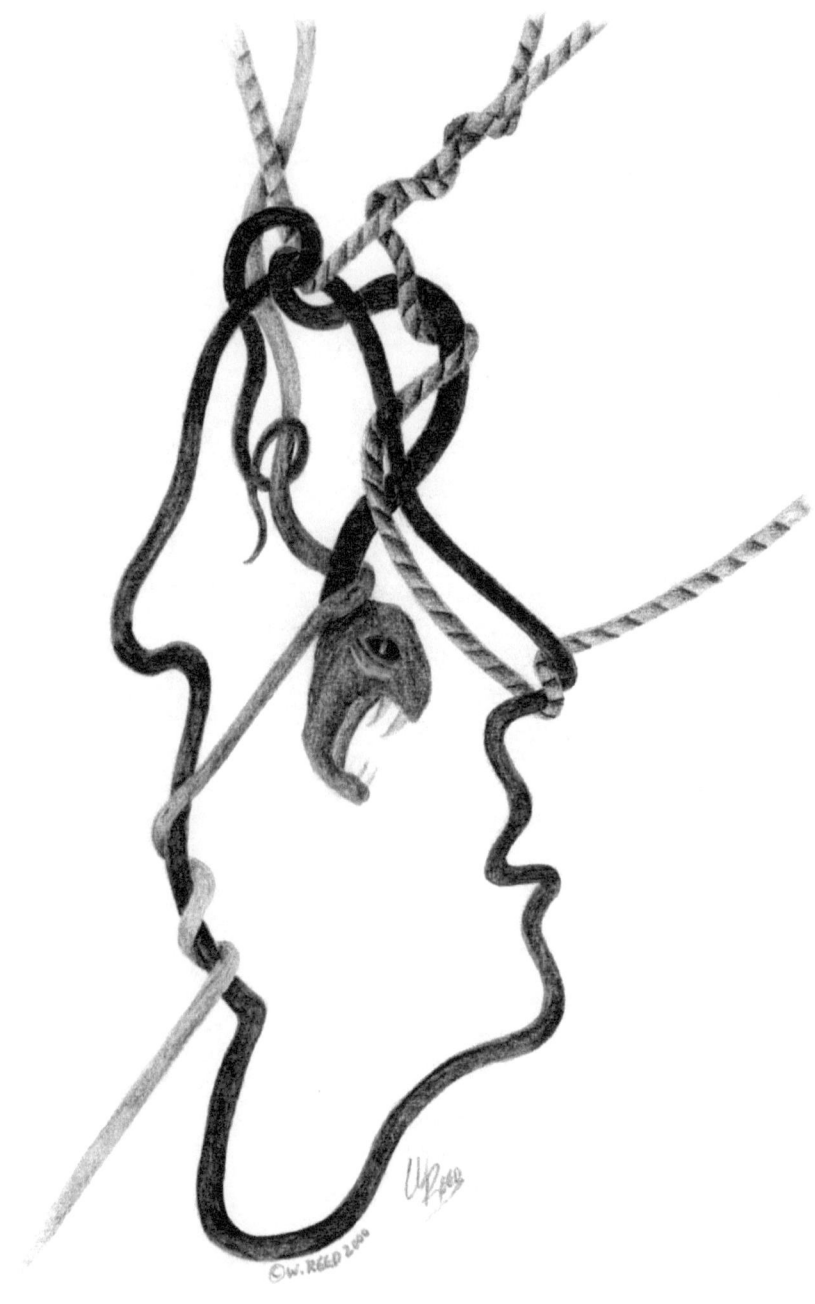

Herman, thinking

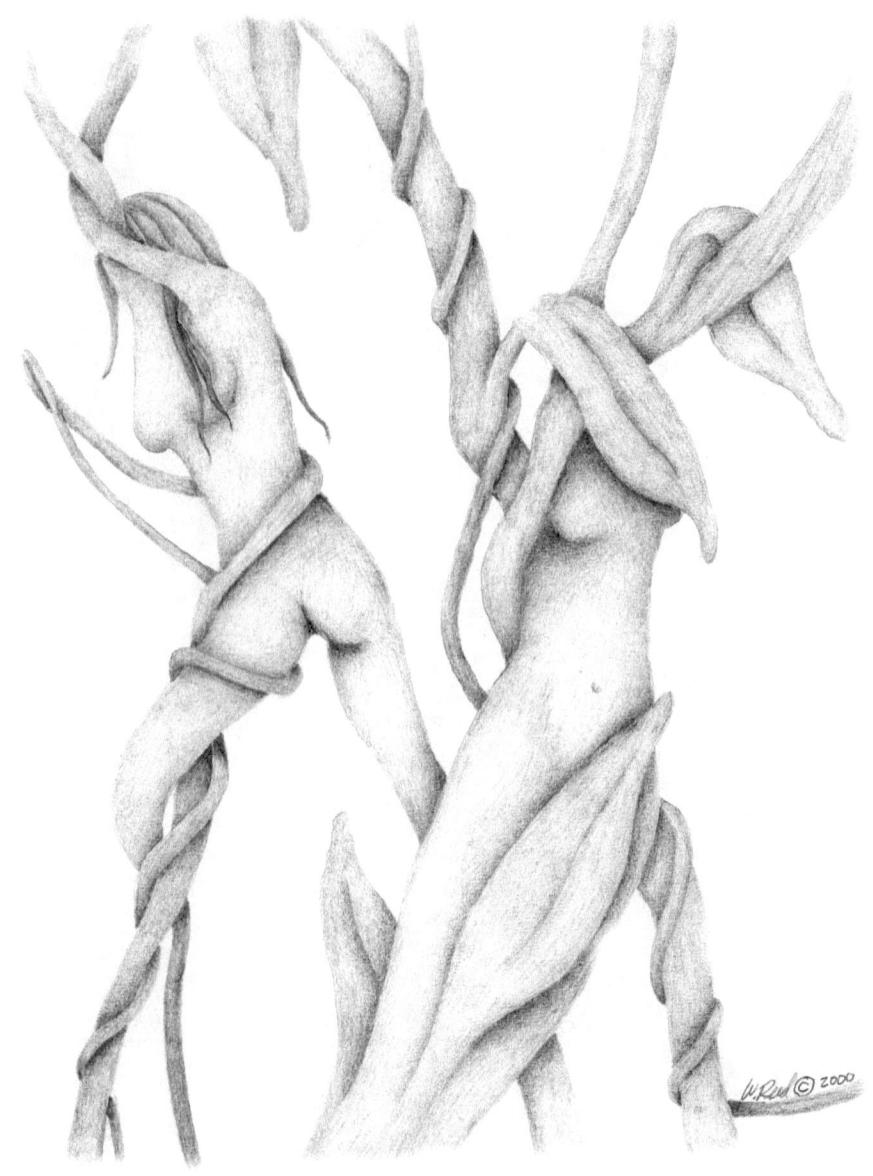

Siblings

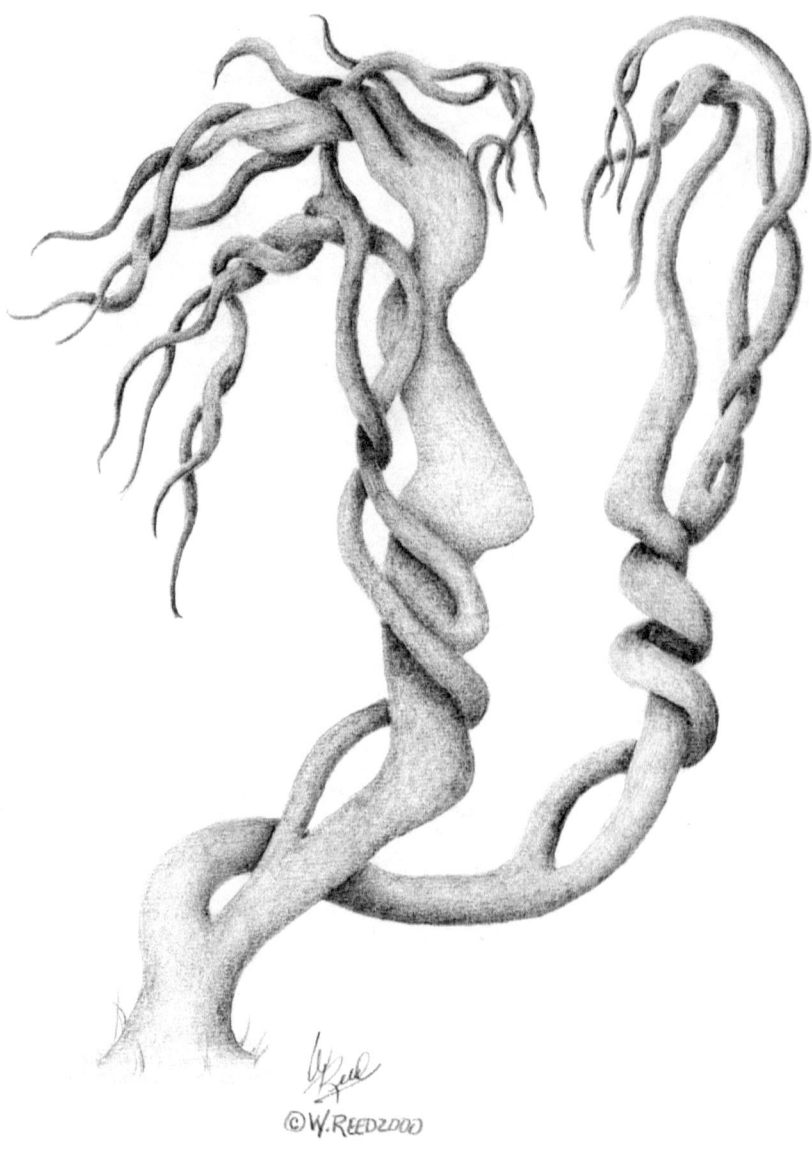

The Kiss

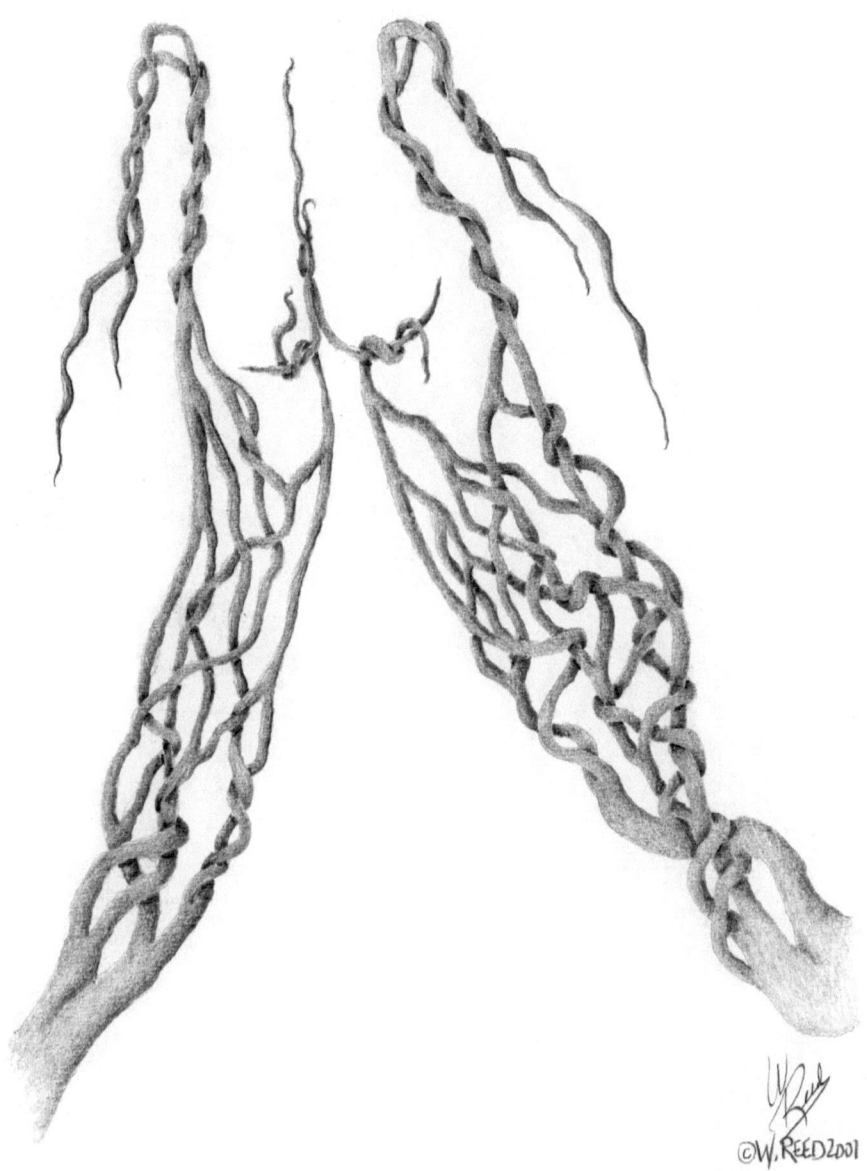

Womens Plight

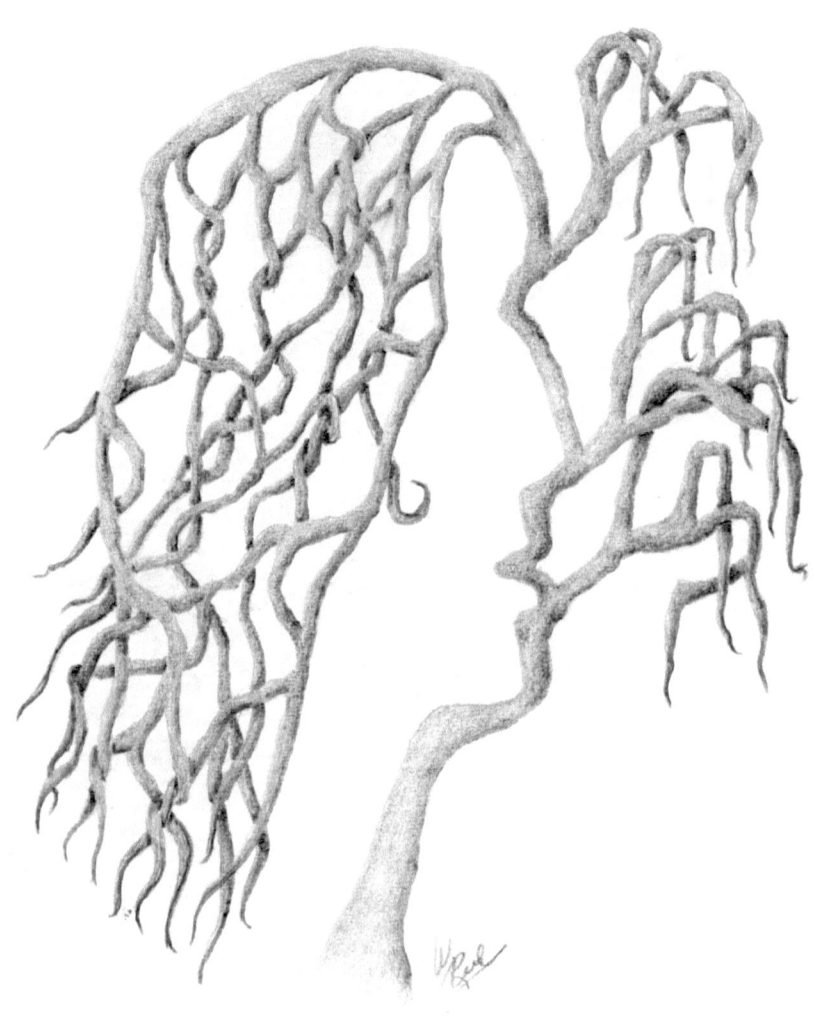

©W.REED 2000

Thought Tree

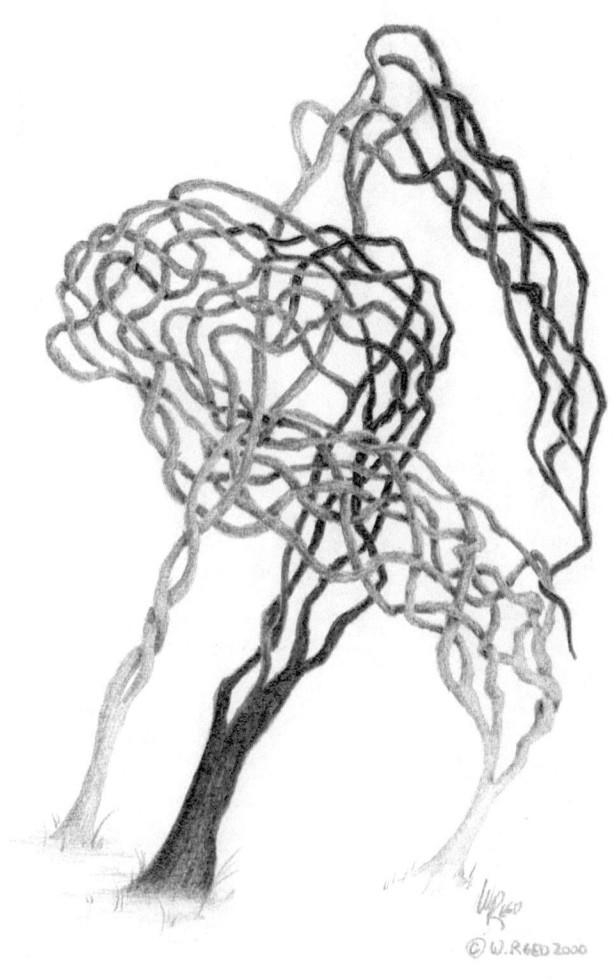

Regrowing Bush

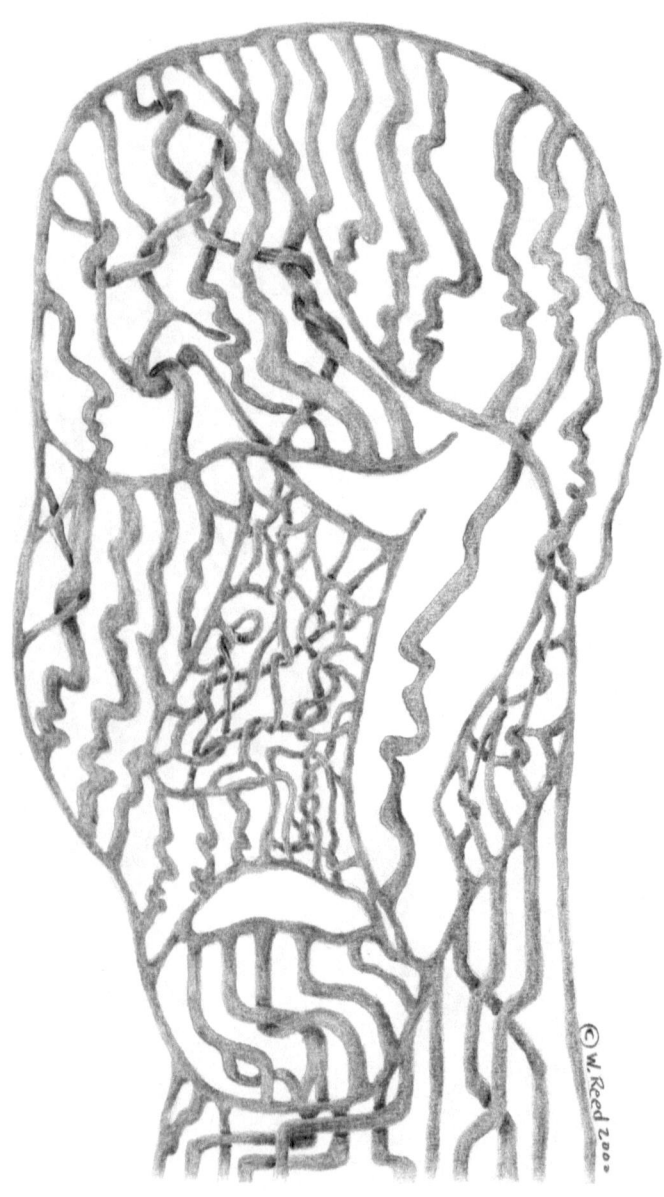

Remembering

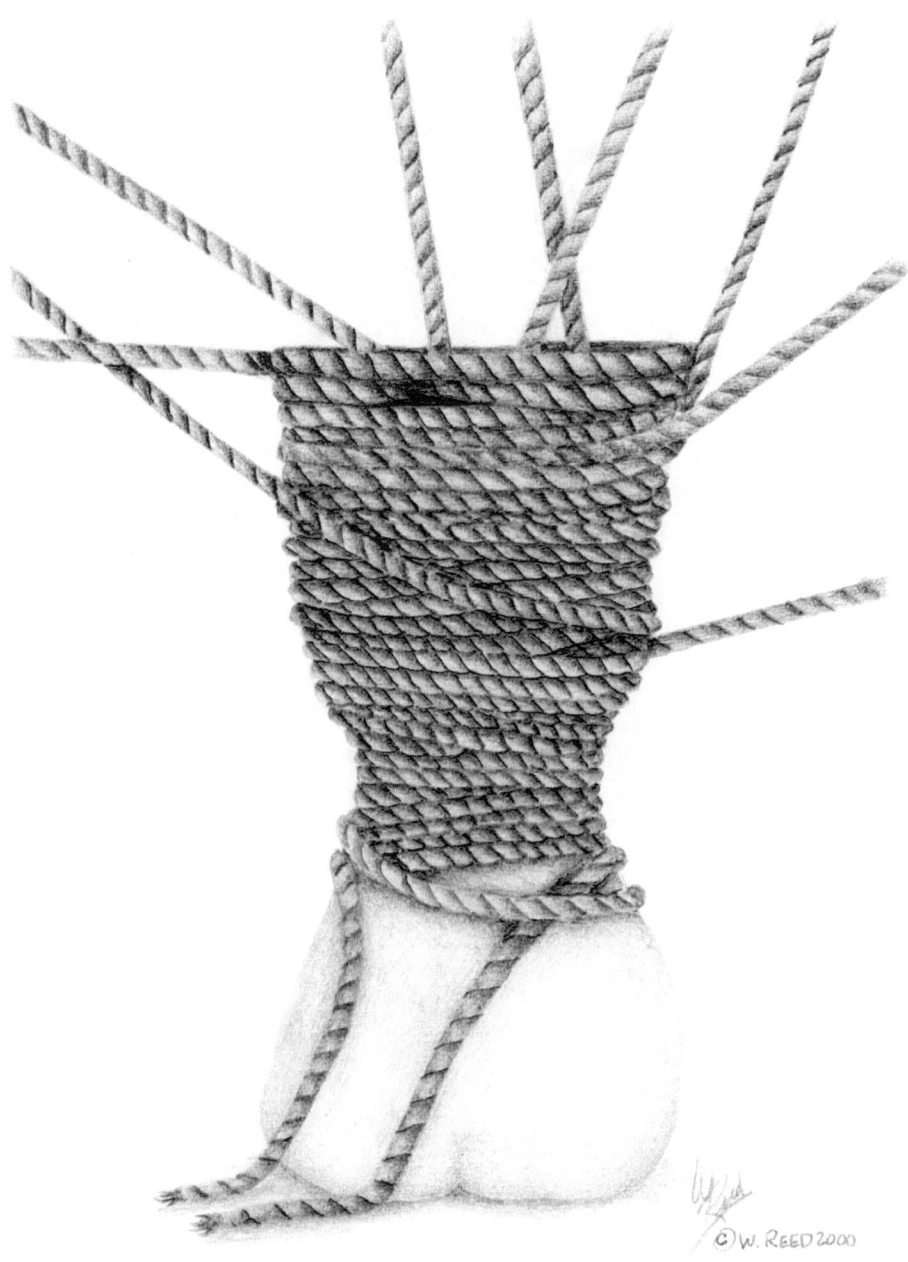

Ega-dnob

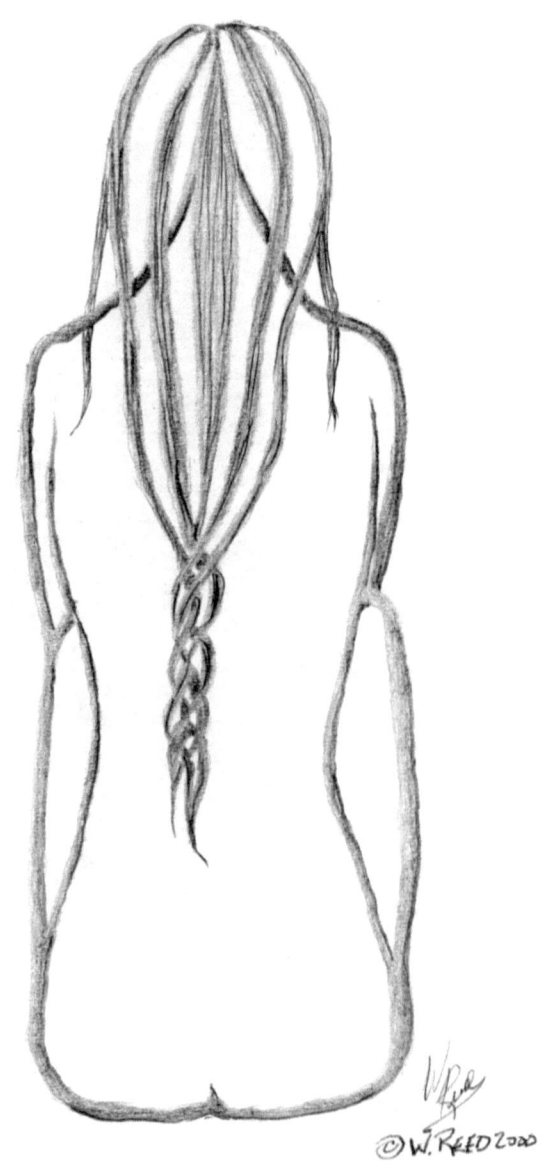

Olivevine

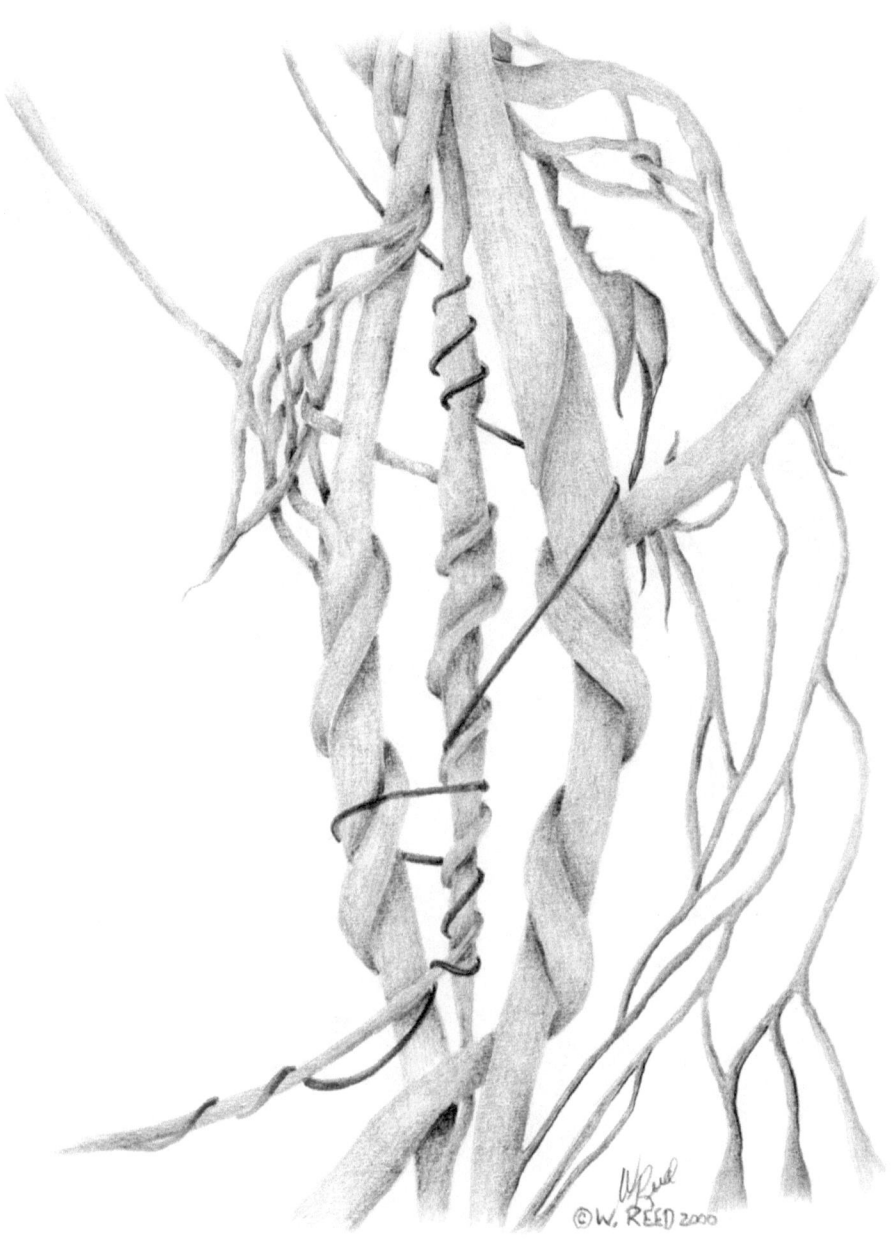

Consouling Sister

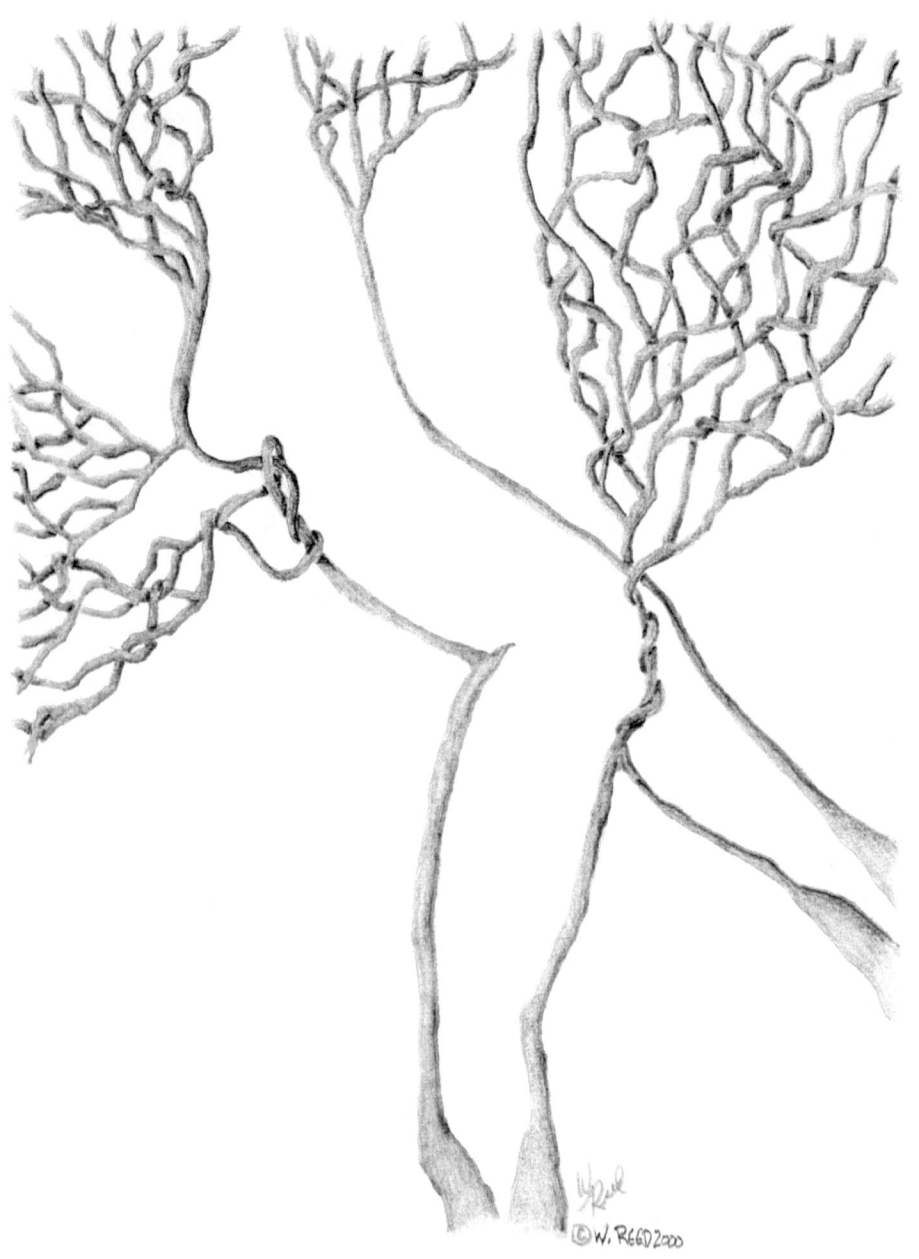

Growing Girl

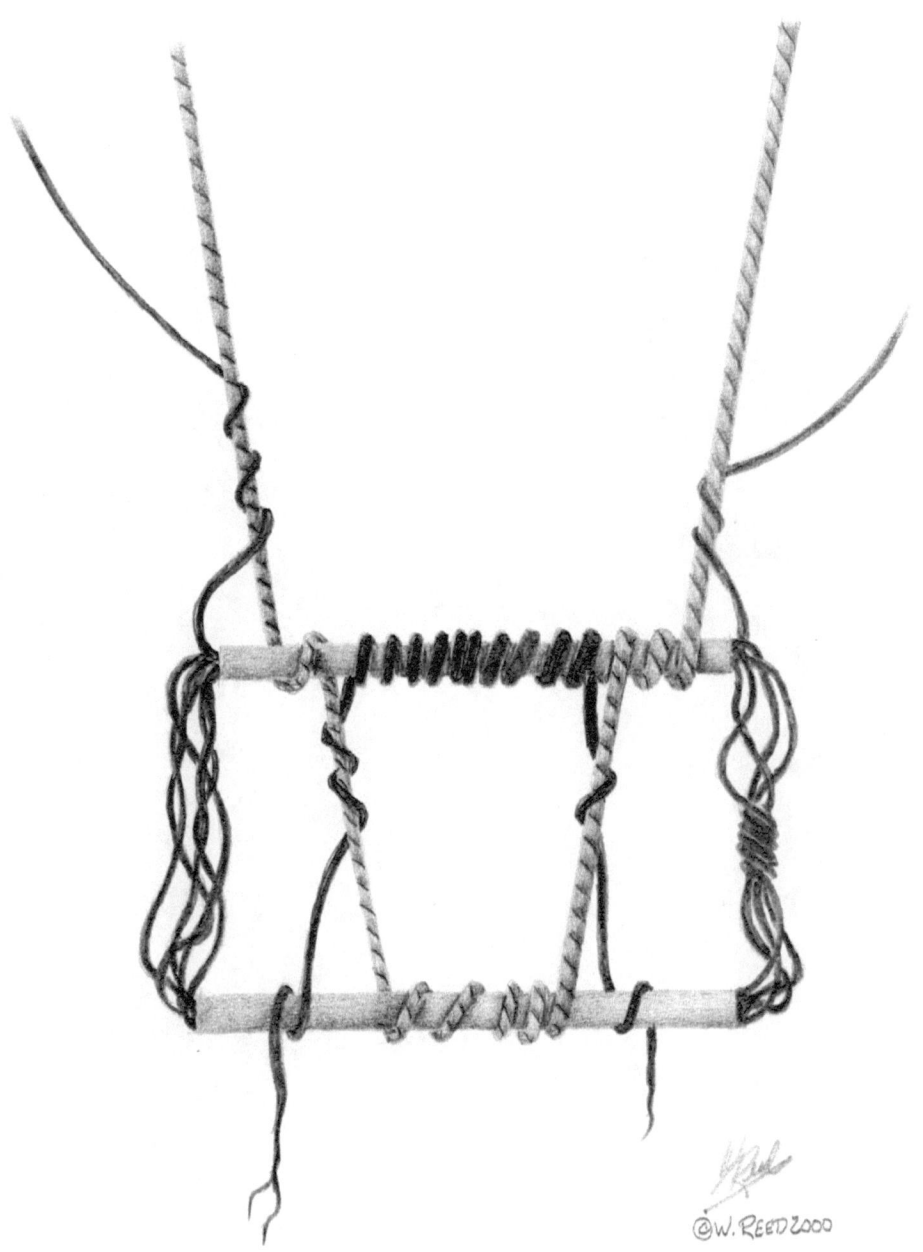

Antenna

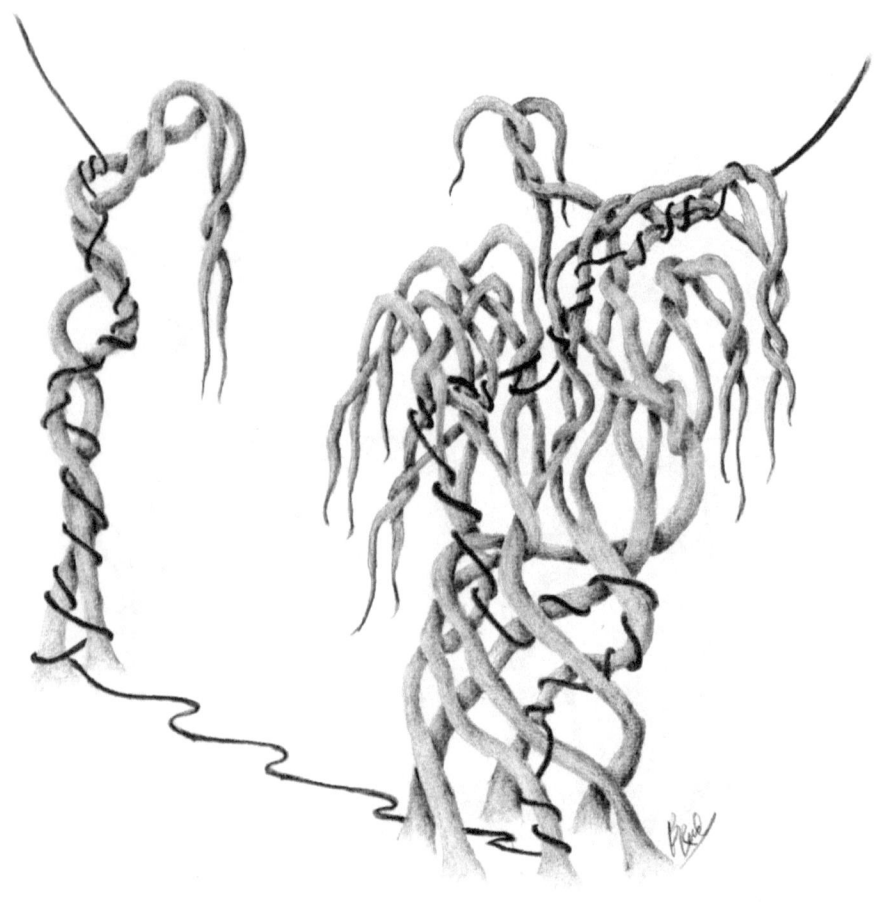

©W. REED 2000

Cable Disfuntion

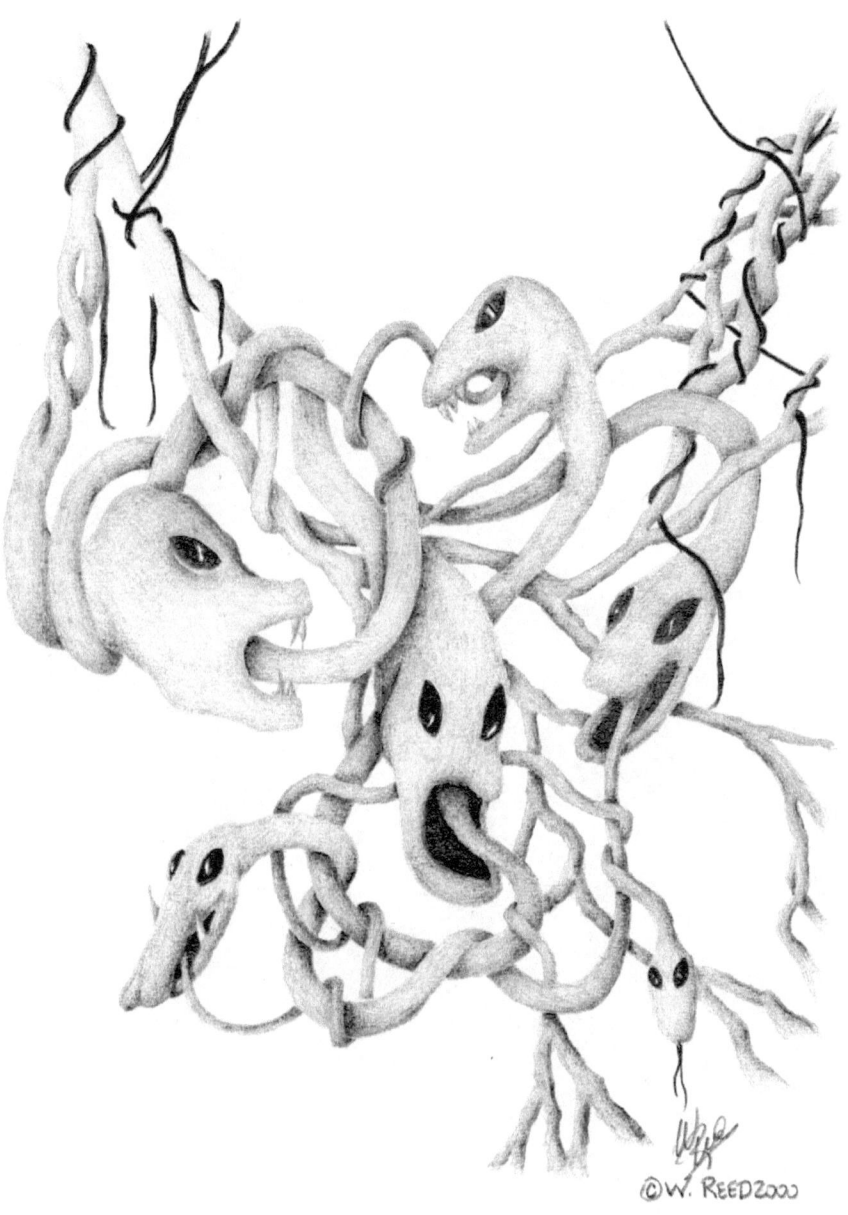

Tongue Twister

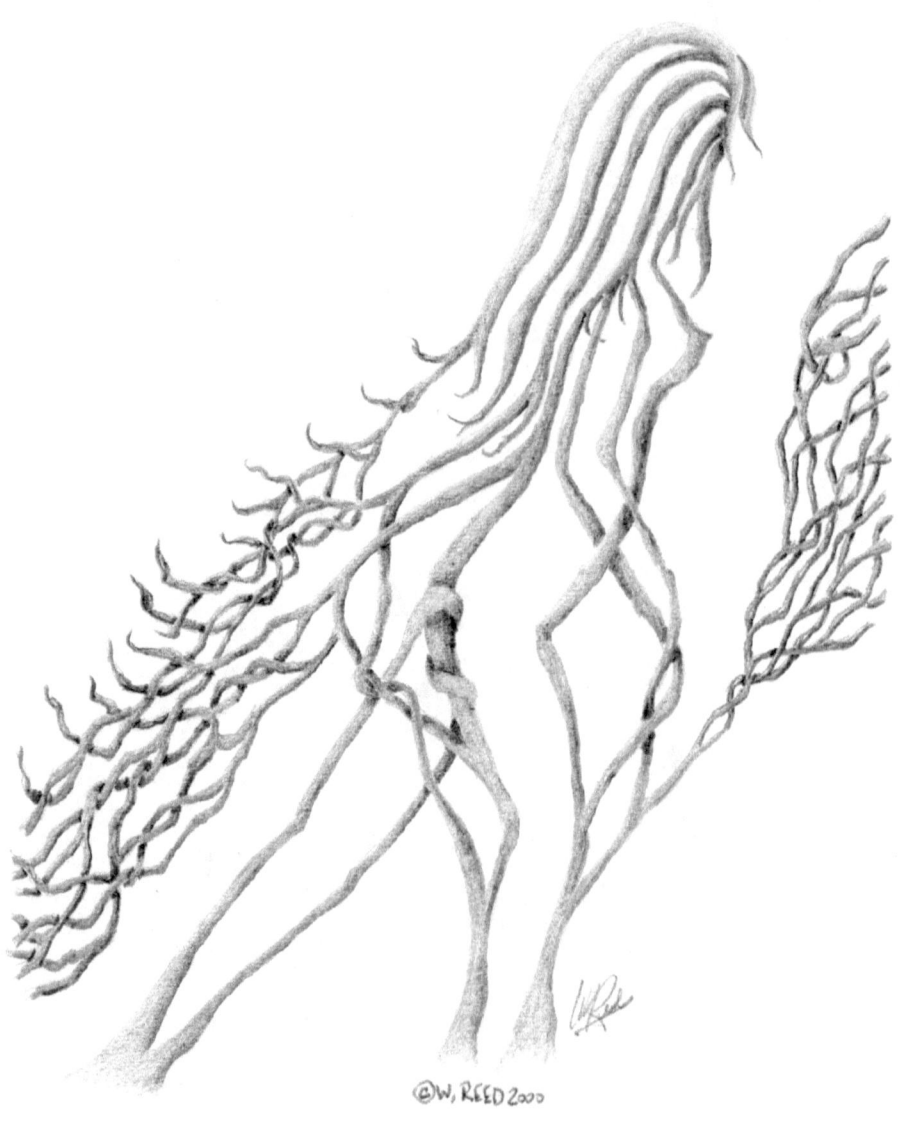

©W. REED 2000

Growing Girl 2

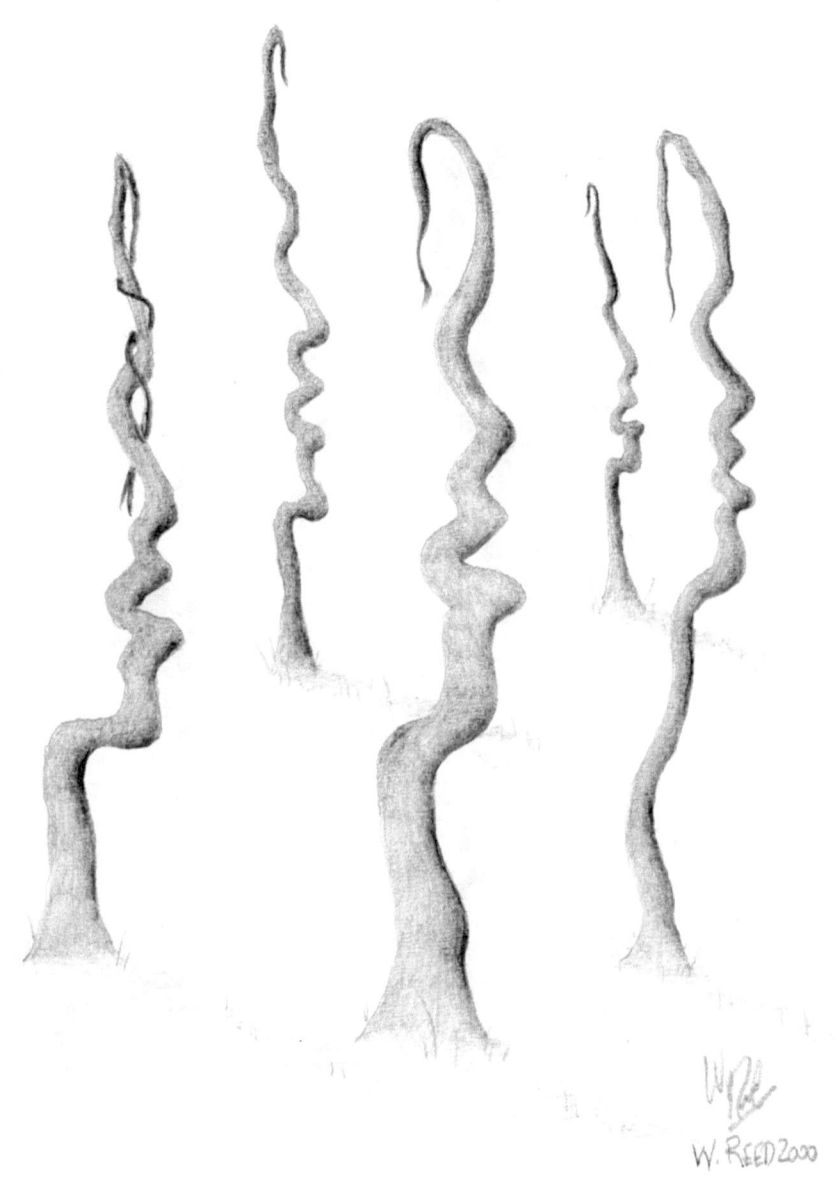

Girl With 4 Brothers

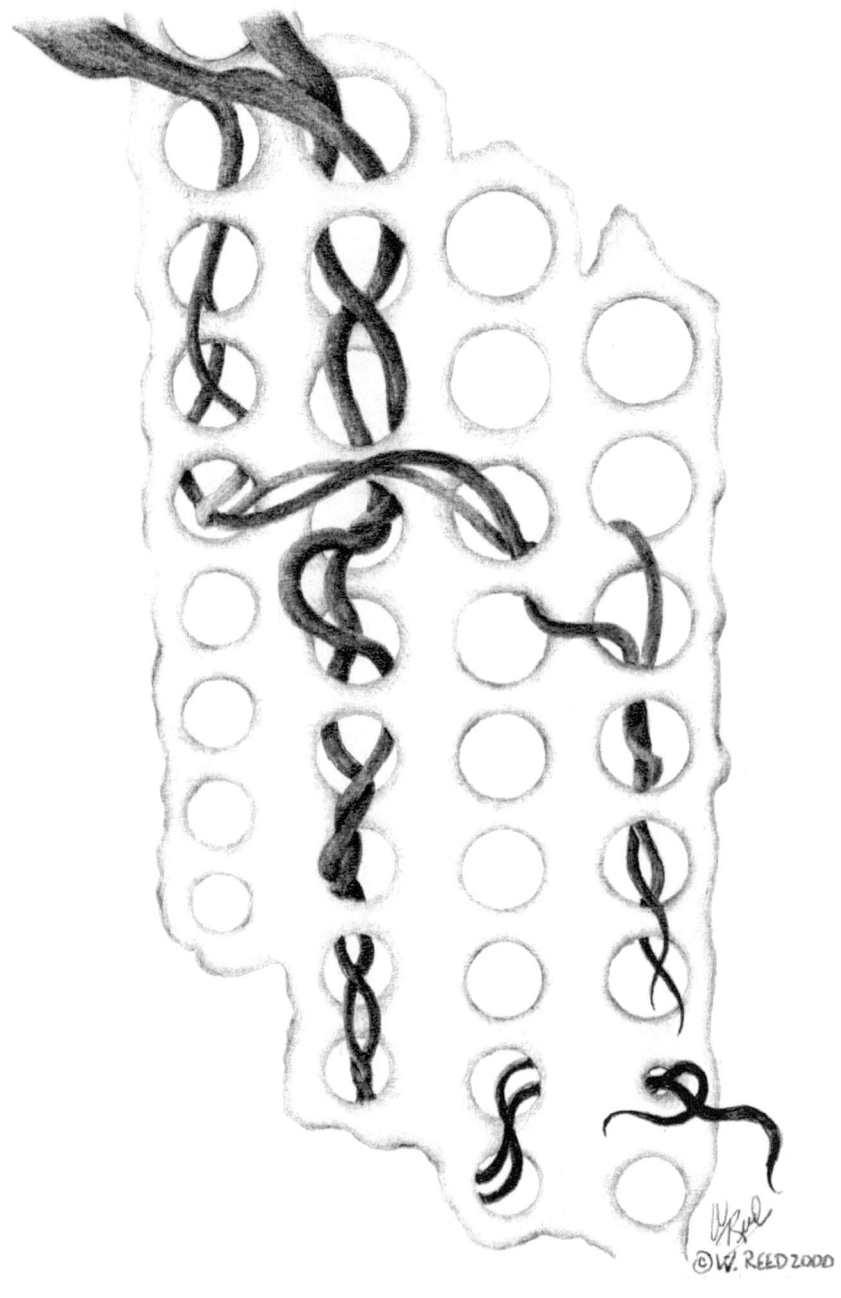

Bad Swiss

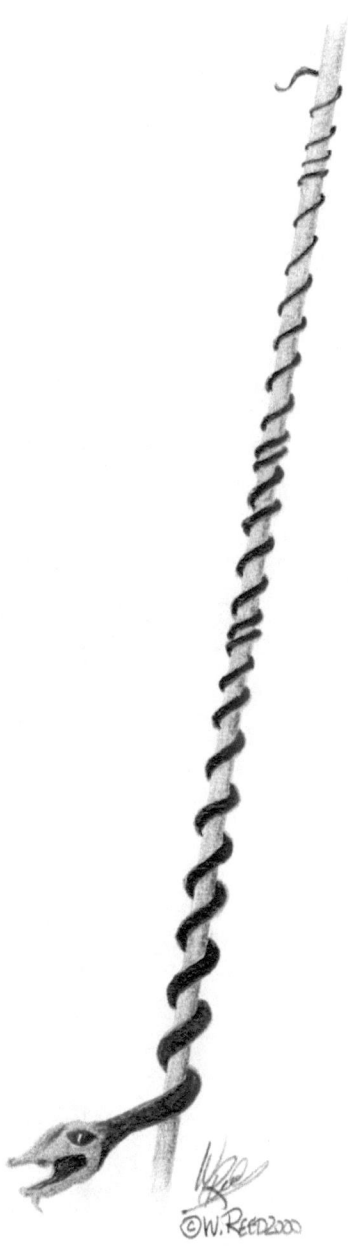

Snake on a Stick

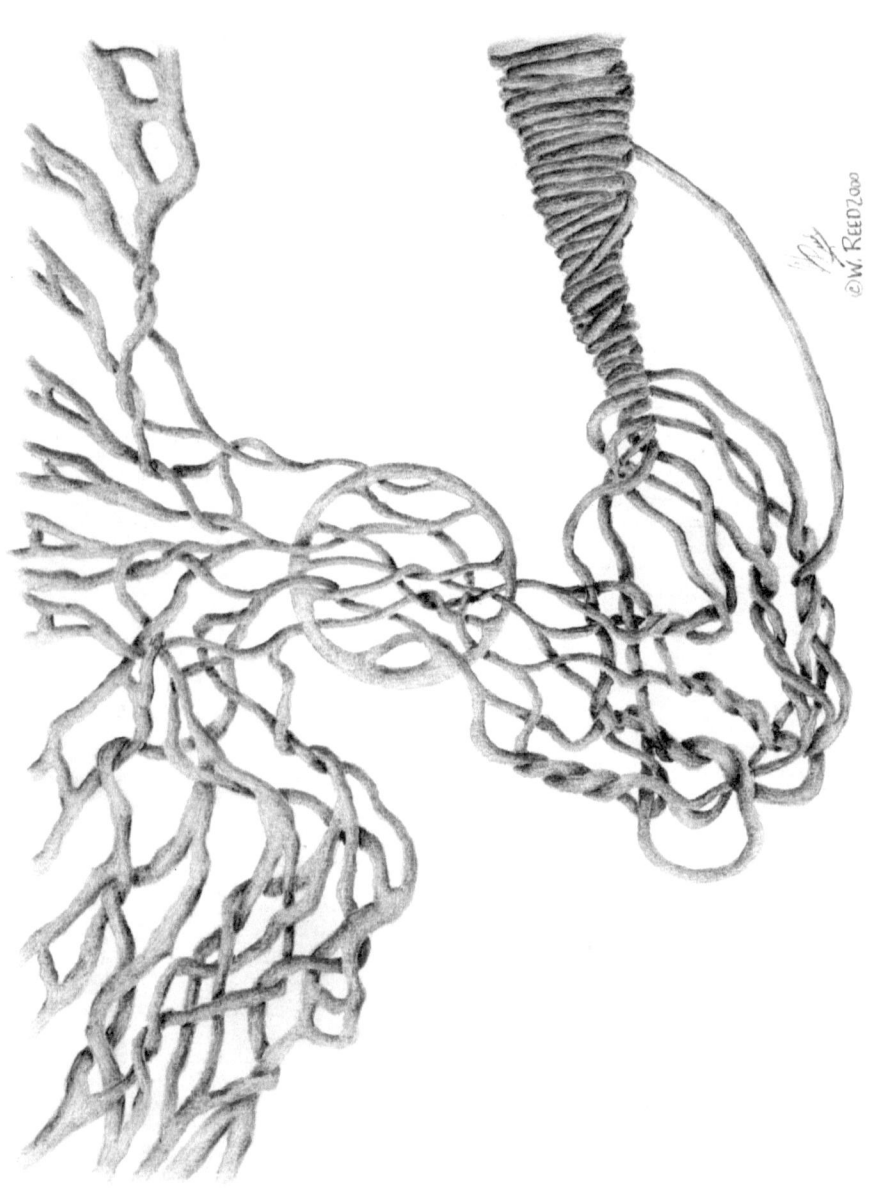

Dream Snatcher

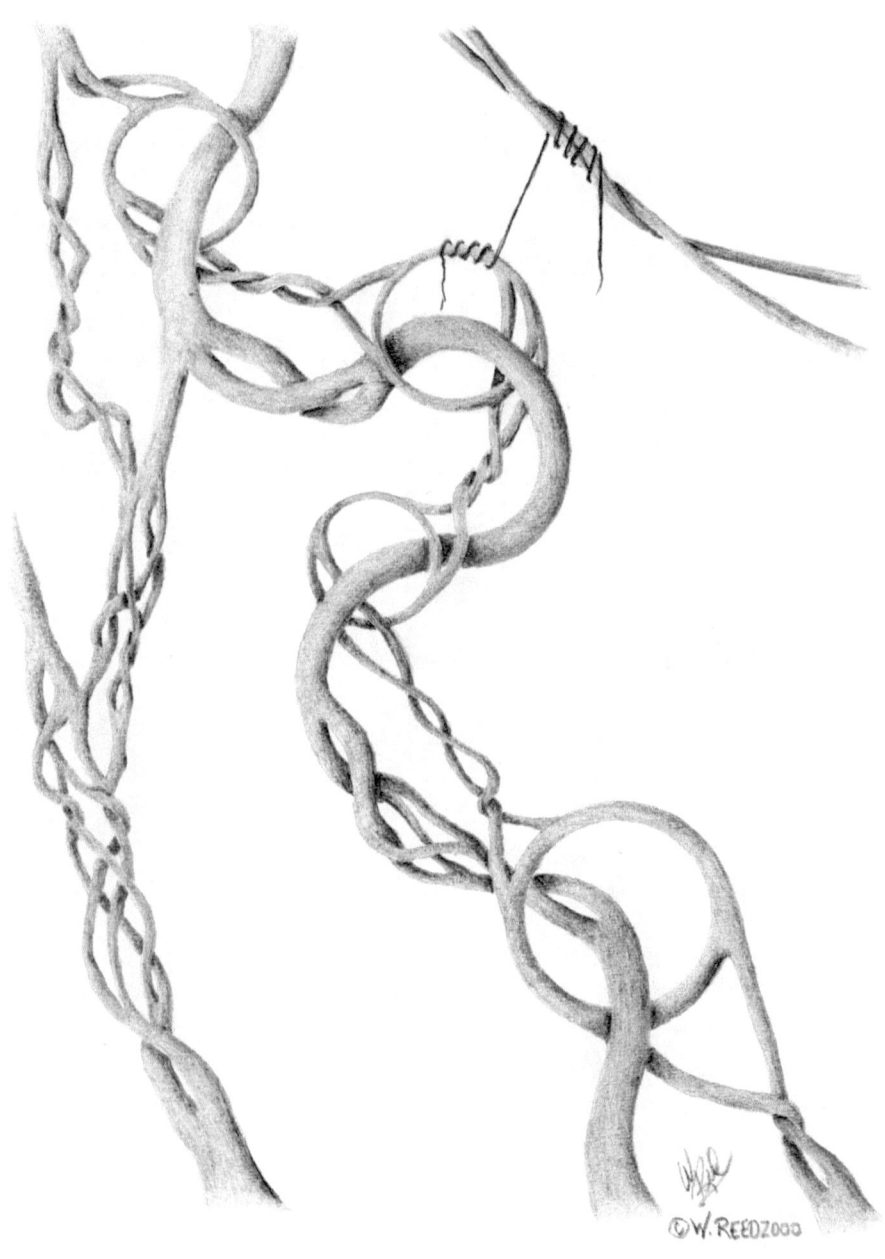

Path of Least Resistance

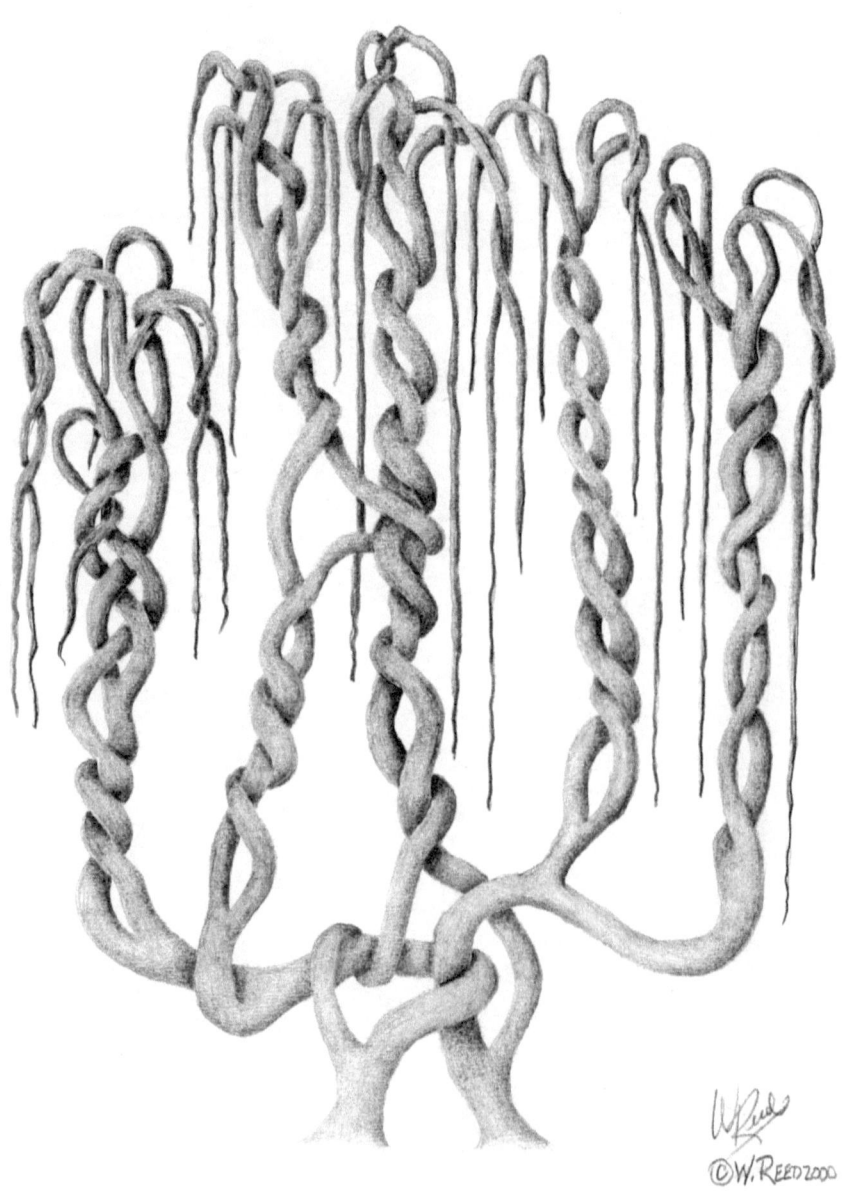

Married with Children

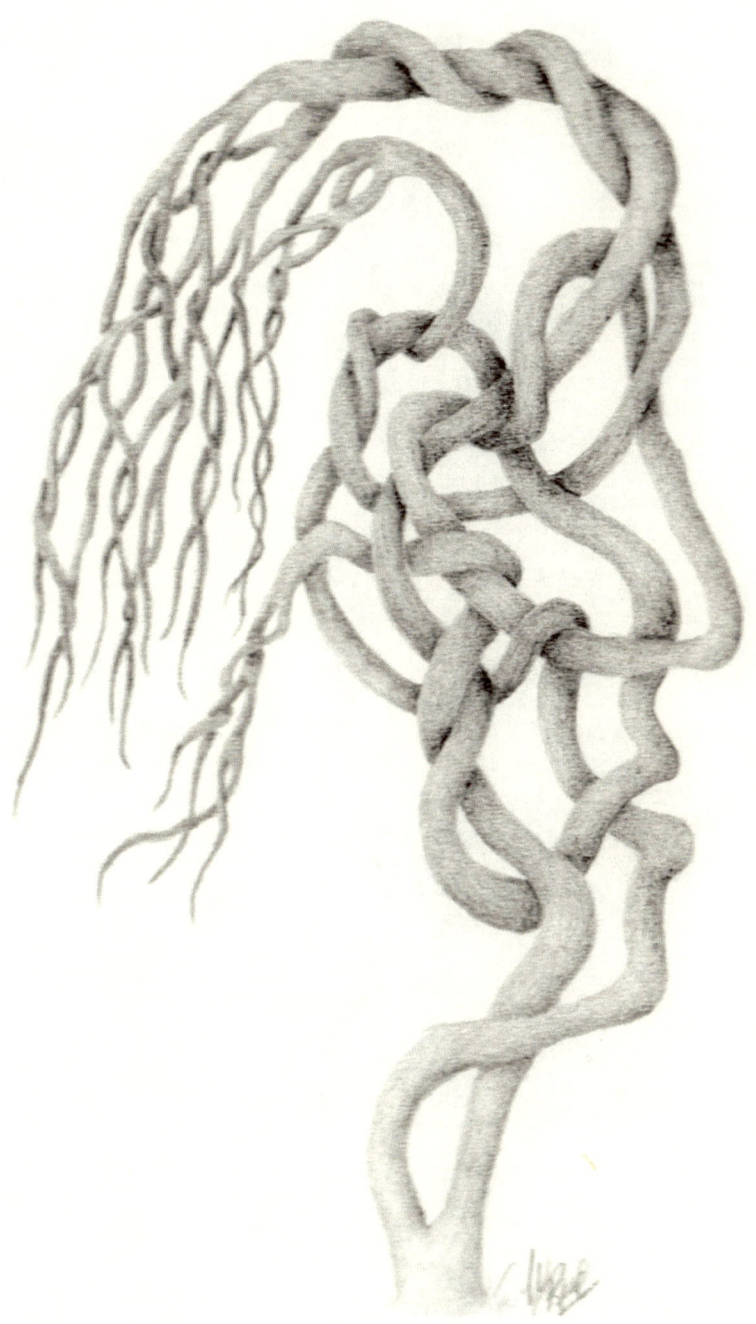

Contemplation Tree

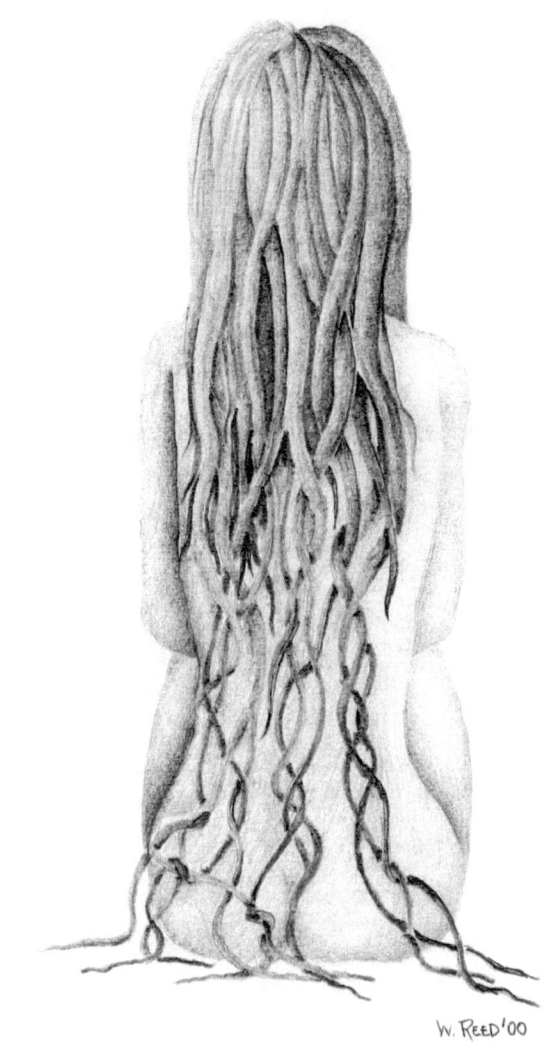

Wondering

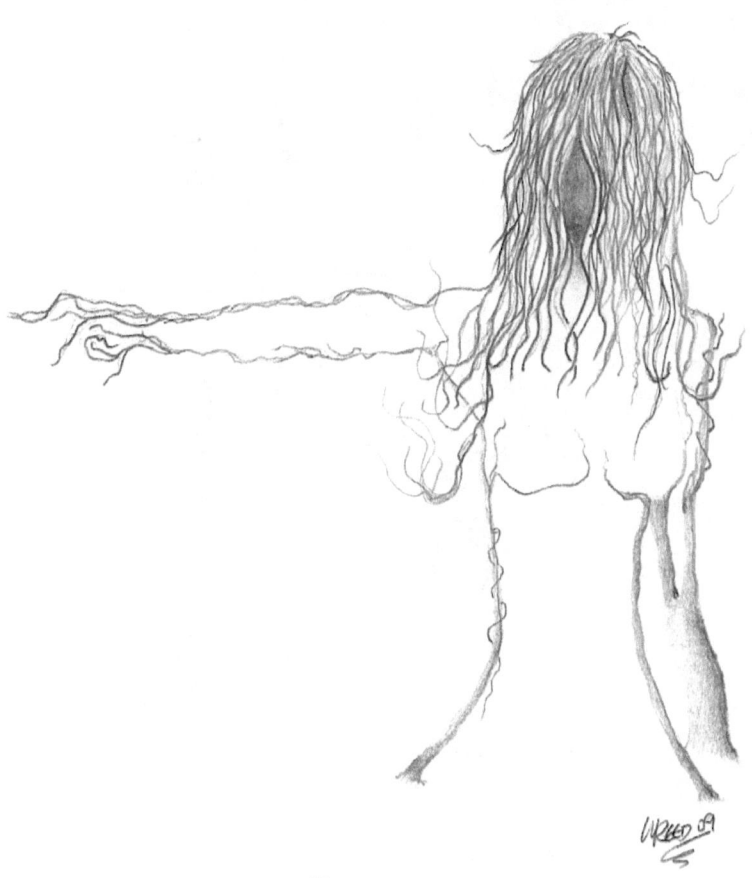

That Away

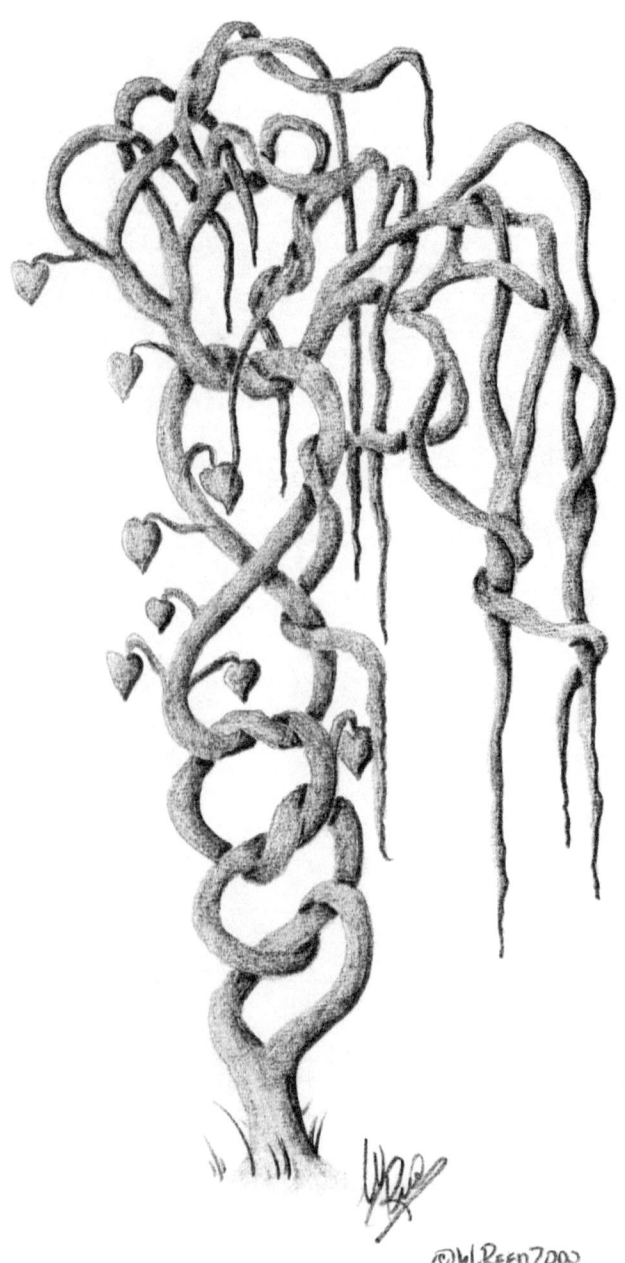

©W.Reed 2000

Tree of Hearts

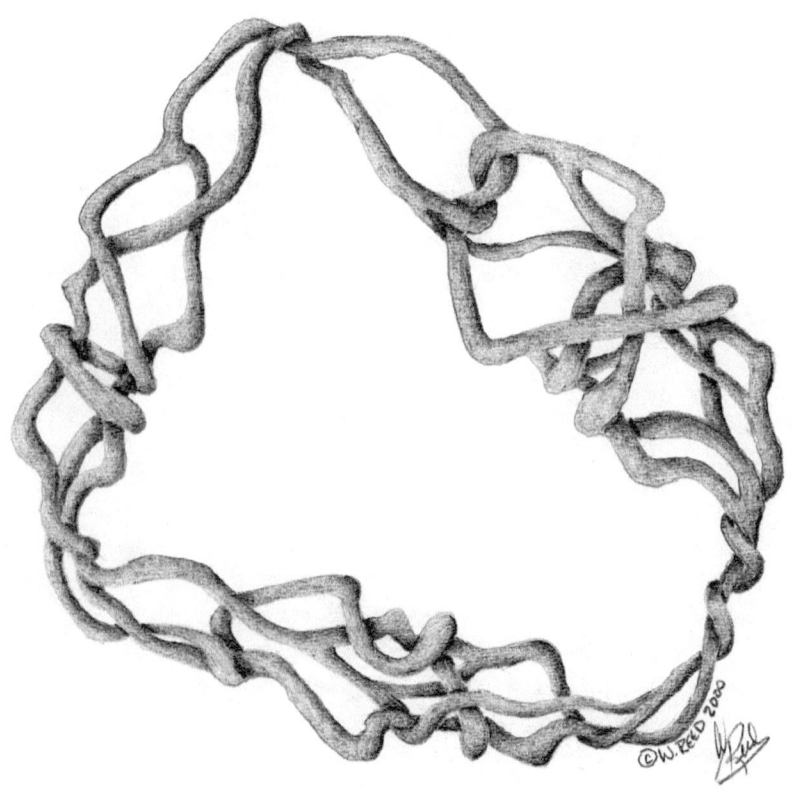

One Thought, Six Views

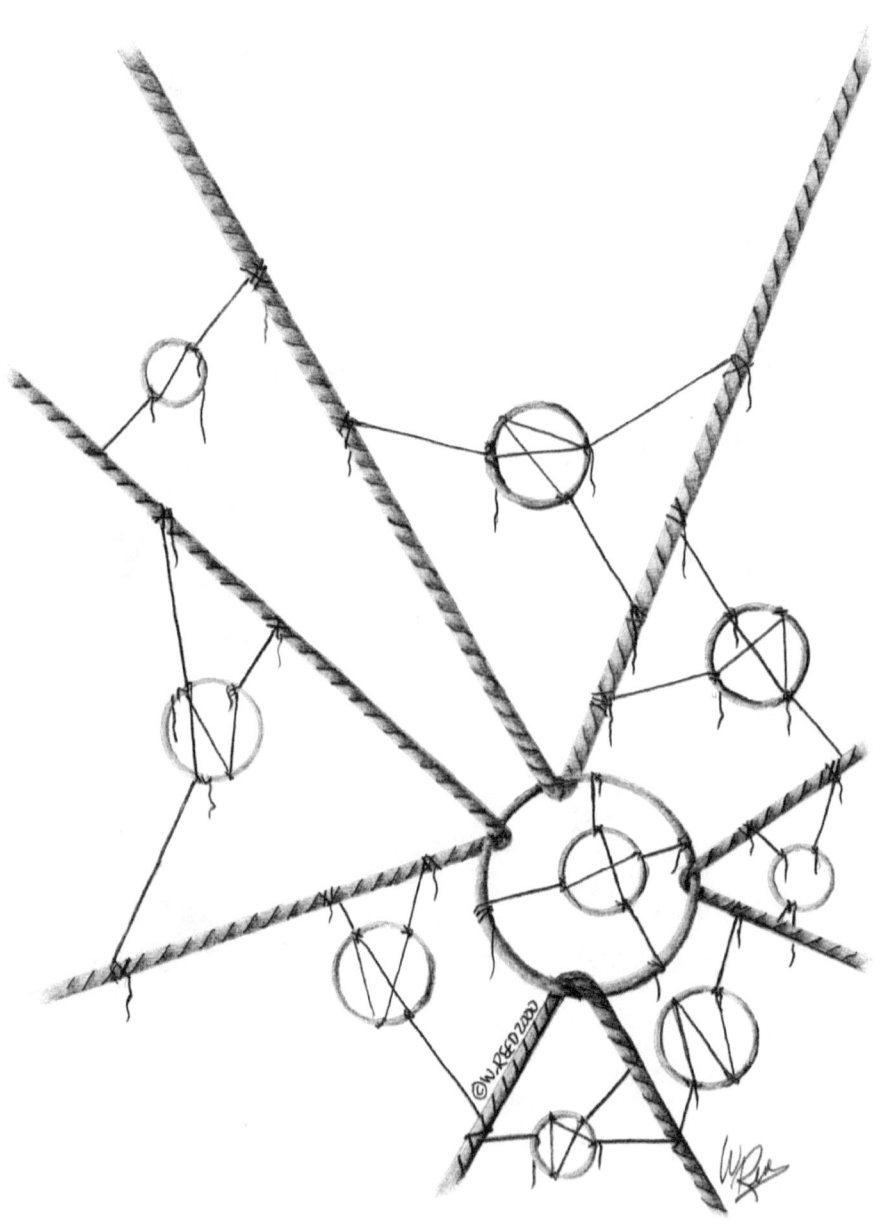

Spider Catcher

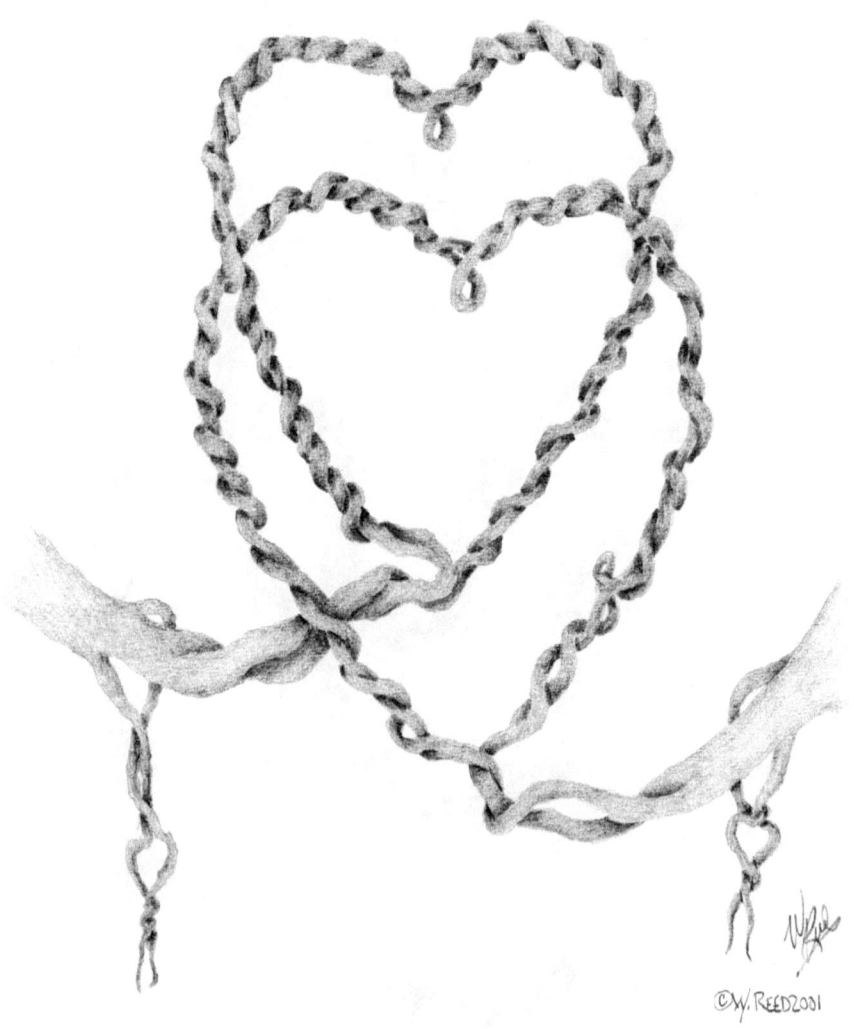

Valentwine

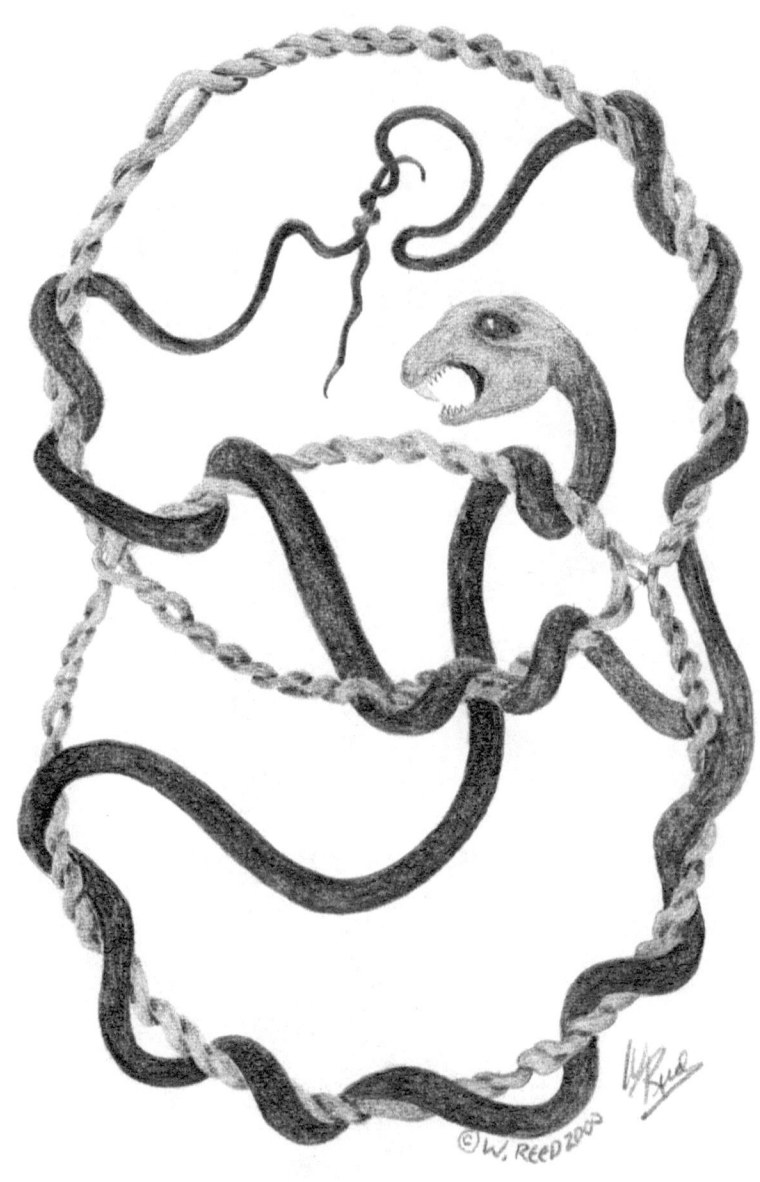

Magic Rings

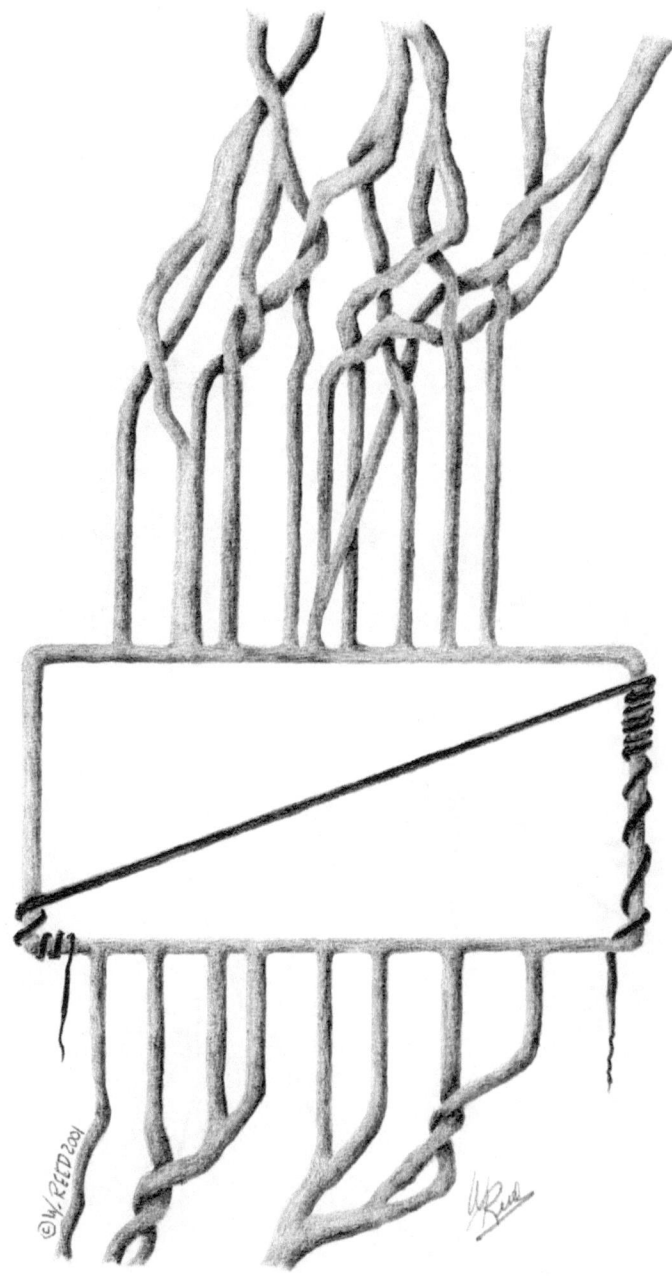

Antenna 2

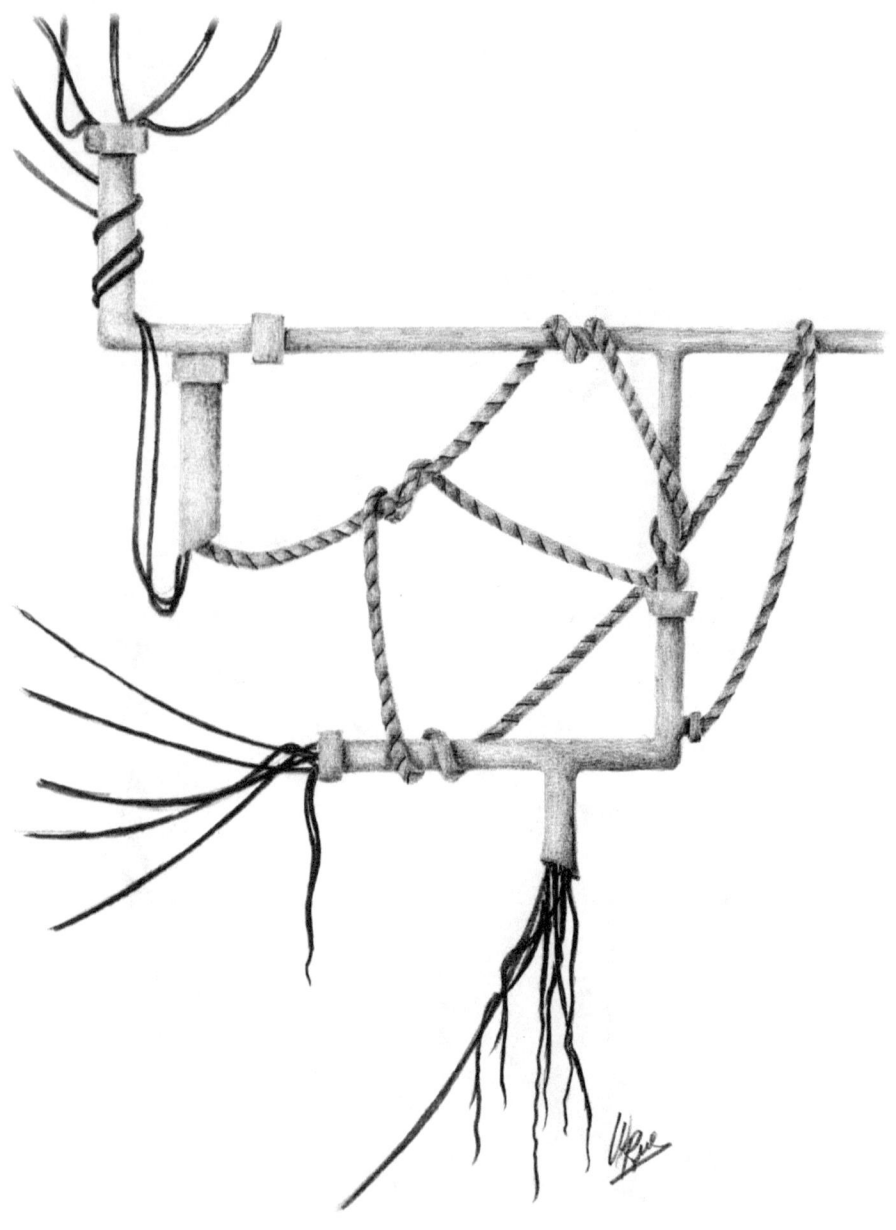

Antenna 3

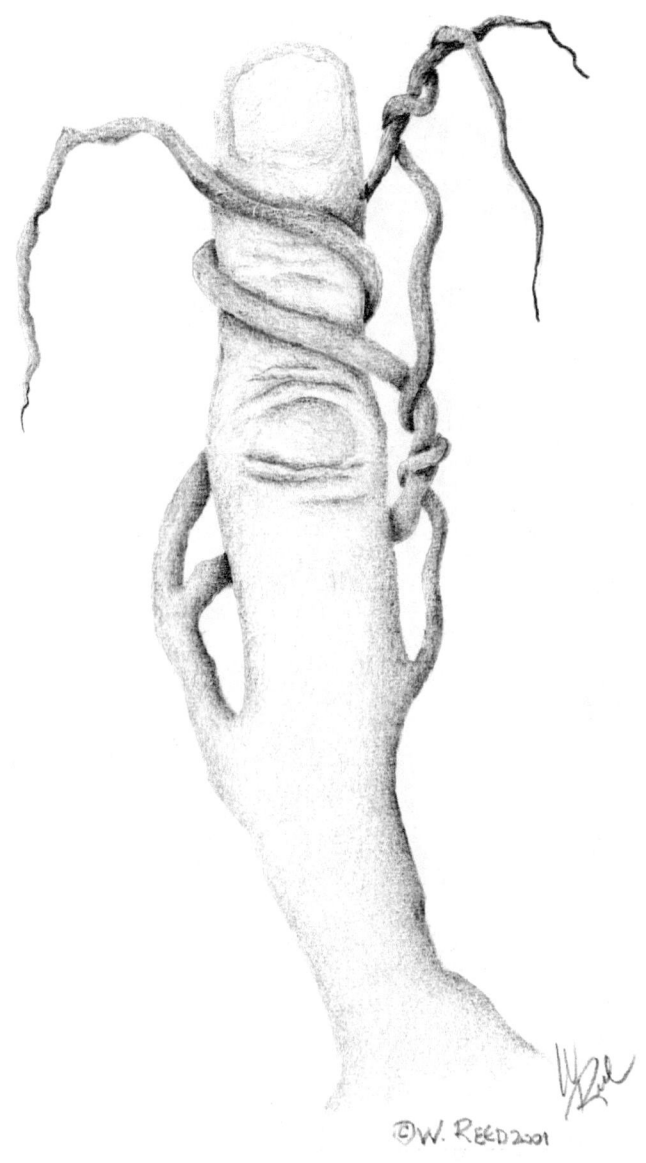

©W. REED 2001

My Finger

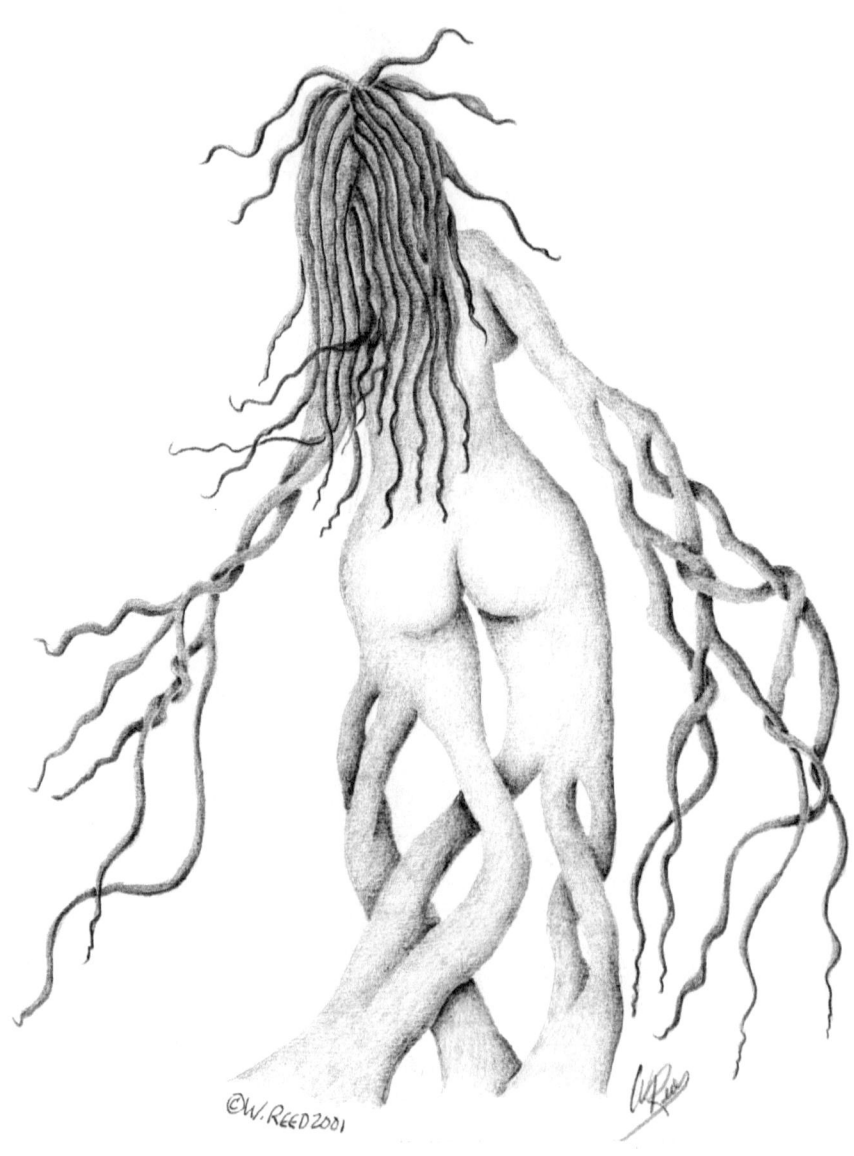

©W.Reed 2001

Jane Growing

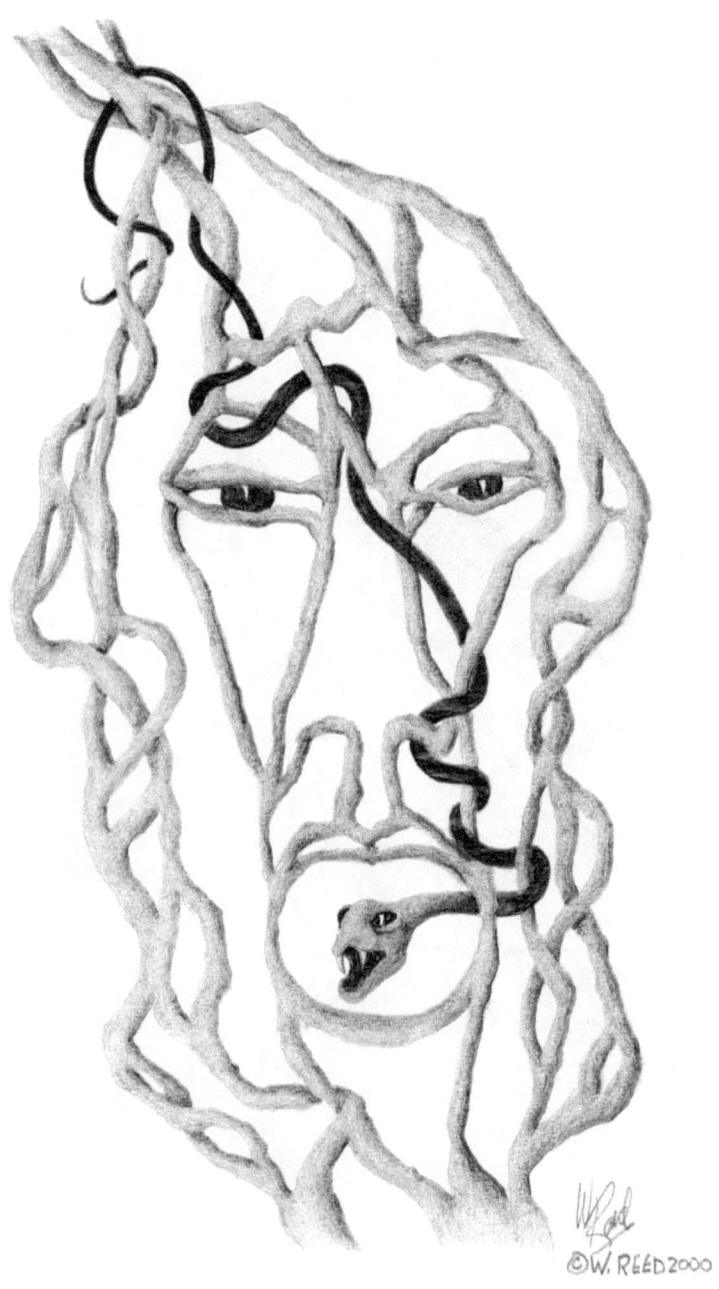

Inside Thoughts

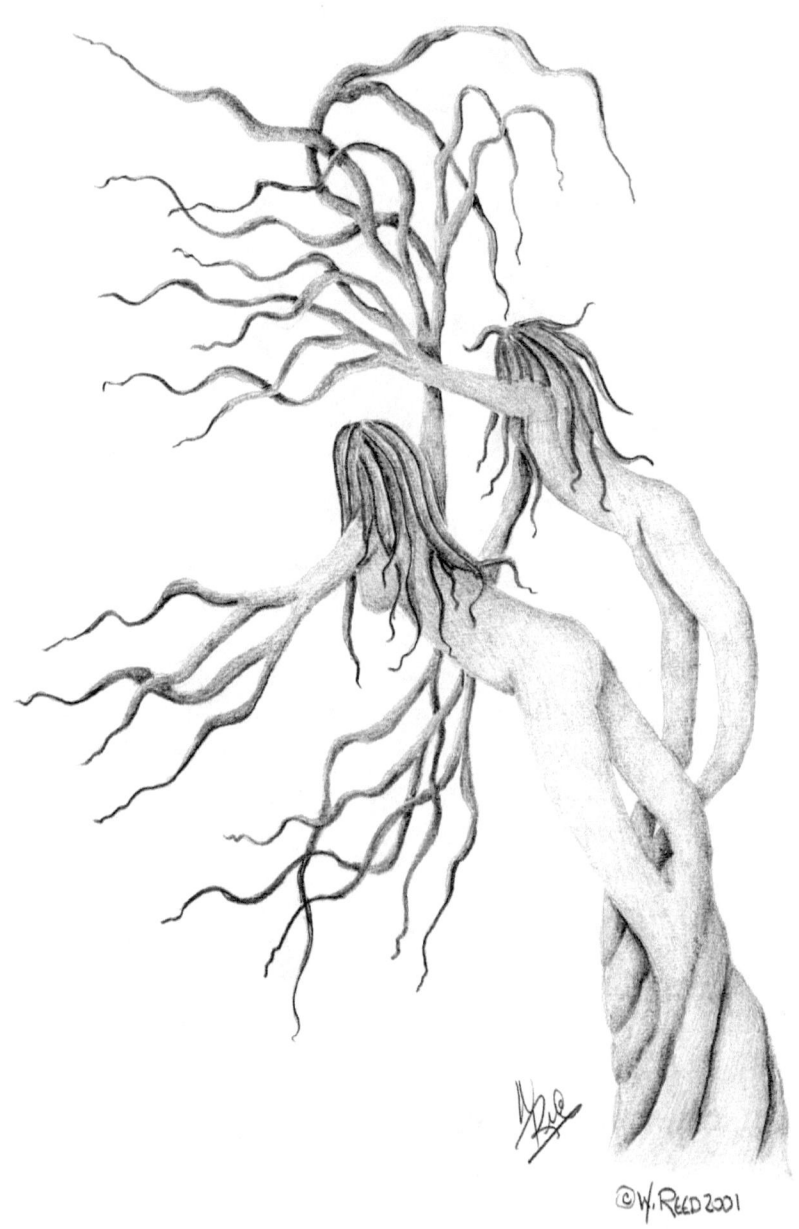

©W. Reed 2001

Disguised

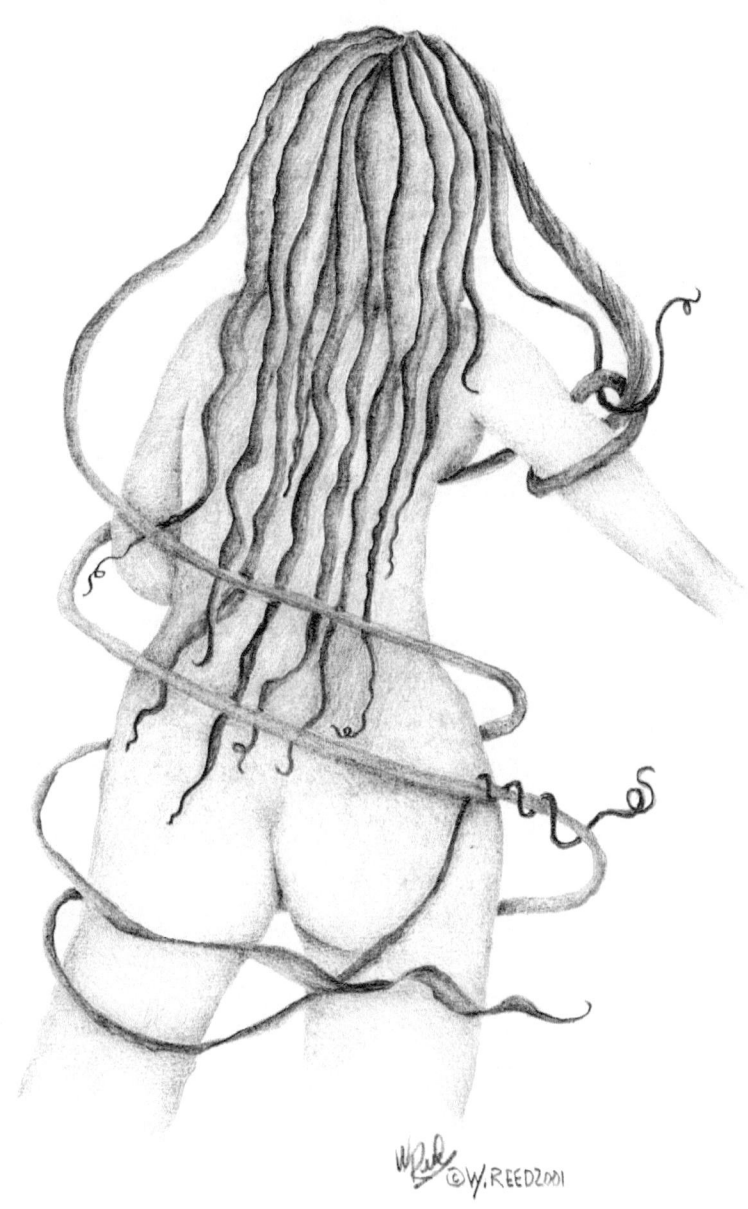

Twisted Sister